ANSWERING THE TOUGHEST QUESTIONS ABOUT HEAVEN AND HELL

ANSWERING THE TOUGHEST QUESTIONS ABOUT HEAVEN AND HELL

BRUCE BICKEL & STAN JANTZ
WITH CHRISTOPHER GREER

BETHANYHOUSE

a division of Baker Publishing Group
Minneapolis, Minnesota

© 2017 by Bruce Bickel and Stan Jantz

Published by Bethany House Publishers
11400 Hampshire Avenue South
Bloomington, Minnesota 55438
www.bethanyhouse.com

Bethany House Publishers is a division of
Baker Publishing Group, Grand Rapids, Michigan

Printed in the United States of America

Library of Congress Cataloging-in-Publication Data
Names: Bickel, Bruce, author.
Title: Answering the toughest questions about heaven and hell / Bruce Bickel and
    Stan Jantz ; with Christopher Greer.
Description: Minneapolis, Minnesota : Bethany House, 2017. | Includes
    bibliographical references.
Identifiers: LCCN 2016036481 | ISBN 9780764218712 (trade paper : alk. paper)
Subjects: LCSH: Heaven—Christianity—Miscellanea. | Hell—Christianity—
    Miscellanea. | Future life—Christianity—Miscellanea.
Classification: LCC BT832 .B53 2017 | DDC 236/.2—dc23
LC record available at https://lccn.loc.gov/2016036481

Cover design by Rob Williams, InsideOutCreativeArts

Authors are represented by The Steve Laube Agency

17 18 19 20 21 22 23   7 6 5 4 3 2 1

Contents

Acknowledgments

Bruce and Stan want to thank Christopher Greer for the work he contributed to this book. In addition to conducting countless personal interviews and designing the surveys, he helped outline and write several chapters.

Bruce, Stan, and Chris want to acknowledge the hundreds of young adults—especially those from St. Andrew's Presbyterian Church in Newport Beach, California—who took the time to articulate their most important questions about heaven and hell. The questions you asked show that you really want to know.

Introduction

Most people enjoy thinking about heaven, even if they don't have good reasons for believing in its existence. Who doesn't want to believe in a place beyond this world where everything will be beautiful and perfect, where there will be no more sorrow or pain or death? The popularity of books about heaven—especially the so-called heaven tourism books written about or by people who supposedly died and went to heaven, only to come back again to tell their story—shows that people are naturally curious about heaven.

Not surprisingly, people don't talk much about hell, unless it's one person telling another person to go there. Even in our churches, the once common "fire and brimstone" message warning people to repent so they won't spend eternity in hell is almost nonexistent. If anything, people prefer to believe that a loving God would never condemn people to a lifetime of torture and agony.

We get that. The idea of God sending people to hell is vexing and complicated. It certainly isn't something you would lead with if you wanted to tell someone why you are a Christian. And if you are still investigating this whole faith in God thing, you probably wouldn't start with hell. So why are we talking about heaven and hell in the same book? Wouldn't it be better to focus on the good part of eternity rather than the bad?

That would be a fine strategy if there were no such place as hell, or if we believed that God would never send anybody there. But what if hell does exist, and what if God has made it pretty clear that there are consequences for not believing and accepting his plan for eternal life in heaven?

These are just two of the many questions we consider in this book about heaven and hell. As we did in our previous book, *Answering the Toughest Questions About God and the Bible,* we relied on Christopher Greer, a pastor who ministers primarily to young adults, to capture the questions people are asking about God, in particular heaven and hell. Although the questions weren't easy to answer, we think the respondents hit the mark. After all, the toughest questions are usually the best.

We have a feeling these would be the kinds of questions you would ask about heaven and hell if we had a chance to speak with you face-to-face. Since we probably won't have the opportunity to ever meet you in person, we hope we have created a space in this book for you to wrestle with these incredibly important issues. Whether you read this book on your own or meet together with a small group, our desire is that you get to know God better and appreciate him more because of what he has planned for you beyond the life you now live.

Bruce Bickel and Stan Jantz

1

Is There an Afterlife?

Introduction

Robert was dying of cancer. His granddaughter, Erin, hoped and prayed that he would turn to God for the first time, put his life in Jesus' hands, and be ready for eternal life. She longed to know she would see her grandfather again someday.

Erin recently began a relationship with God through Jesus, and she grew more and more curious about life after death. Her grandfather was never so interested in God or the afterlife. As an atheist, he believed there was no God and that life—the moments packed between our first and last breath—is all there is. For Robert, life was restricted to the immediate, the here and now, the physical and material. When death comes, the movie is finished, the credits role, and then all fades to black. Nothing awaits us. There is no sequel. And the rest of the world goes on.

When Robert died, Erin's cousin (who is agnostic about God) tried to comfort her. She said, "Erin, Grandpa Robert lived well, and we can be thankful that now there is nothing for him. No more pain, no more anything. He would be glad we have our memories to look back on." Erin agreed that living a good life was very important, but her cousin's words were far from comforting. Erin could not help but believe there was more to life than this.

As she grieved her beloved grandfather's death, she wrestled with what might or might not lie ahead. Is there life after this one? Is this life—this physical world and our experiences in it—all there is? Or are her newfound belief and her gut-level intuition correct in concluding there is plenty more life to be had after this one?

◾ ▓ ◾

When it comes to Erin's question, "Is there life after this?" Christianity answers a resounding *yes!* In fact, the promise of life after death is one of Christianity's key doctrines. For better or worse, one way Christians have tried to begin conversations with others about faith in Jesus is by asking a basic (though somewhat jarring) question: "If you died today, do you know where you would go?" We've always wanted someone to pose that question to one of us so we could coolly reply, "To the morgue."

But we digress.

Have you ever been asked that question? Have you ever been given the life-after-death pop quiz by an eager evangelist at the beach, in a church service, or on an airplane (one of the *least* appropriate and most anxiety-producing places to bring up death, by the way)? The underlying assumption in the zealous inquirer's question about your postdeath destination is that there *is in fact* a postdeath destination. Be it heaven or hell, Christians claim everybody's headed somewhere. The promise of heaven is, in part, what intrigues Erin about Christianity, and it gives her hope as she mourns for her grandfather and wrestles with the sorrow, pain, and uncertainty of life.

But are belief-colored glasses the only way to see a postdeath future? Or are there other road signs that point in the same mysterious direction? Later we'll take a close look at what Christianity teaches, but first, let's see who else is talking about life after death. As it turns out, Christians are not alone on this one.

The 99 Percent

Have you ever boldly expressed an opinion only to find you're the only one who holds it? It happens to us more than you know! This, believe it or not, is the experience of those who say there is no life after death. Though Erin's grandfather and cousin are two key players in this chapter's opening story, they are part of a small minority of people in world history who don't believe in a postdeath reality. Today the trend continues. Though there are pockets of disbelief around the world, the large majority of people believe in life after death. It's important to note that this fact neither solves the afterlife enigma nor dismisses it. It's simply a fact, one that is helpful to know as we explore honestly whether or not there is life after this one. What follows is a breakdown that reveals the ubiquity of the belief in life, of one kind or another, after death.

In the Old, Old Days

Belief in the afterlife was as prevalent centuries ago as it is today. In Alan Segal's comprehensive history of the afterlife in Western religion, he notes: "Notions of afterlife are universal in human experience; indeed, they are older than human life, if Neanderthal grave sites are taken as evidence."[1] For millions of years tombs have been built to house dead bodies *and* various accoutrements (jewelry, tools, everyday utensils, food, decorations, and weapons) believed necessary for navigating the afterlife. The earliest tombs were in the deceased's homes, and they evolved into the remarkable pyramids of ancient Egypt. The question for those cultures—going as far back as the Stone Age—was not *if* there was an afterlife, but rather how to equip and prepare a person for it.[2] Anthropologists can't say for sure if humanity's oldest ancestors were religious, but the nature of their burial sites leaves little doubt that they believed their dead relatives were not finished living.

What Do the World's Major Religions Say?

The same is true for those in the world who *are* religious: Life after death is a slam dunk. Since their beginning, the great world religions—Christianity, Islam, Judaism, Hinduism, Buddhism, and all their variations—have expressed belief in one of two basic distinctions of the afterlife. Western religion teaches resurrection of the body, while Eastern religion believes souls are reunited with a transcendent ultimate reality. Our intention is not to describe the myriad intricacies found in this planet's religions, but here's a snapshot of what the major ones believe about the hereafter:

Buddhism

Buddhists affirm two options: transmigration (reincarnation) or nirvana. With transmigration, one's spirit (or soul) inhabits another physical body; life after death is really life after life. But the true goal is nirvana. Nirvana is the extinction of desire, through which the spirit of the self is united with the highest state of consciousness. Afterlife then, whether it is rebirth into another living creature or reaching the ultimate, unified consciousness of Buddha, is important in Buddhism.

Hinduism

The afterlife in Hinduism is also rooted in reincarnation. A person's self, or spiritual essence, is believed to be divine and is on a cyclical journey of birth and rebirth. The goal in each life is to attain *moska*, or total liberation from the life and death cycle. Similar to Buddhism, moska is nirvana, or ultimate union with Brahman, the divine. *The Bhagavad Gita*, India's enduring religious work, says this about the self: "Never the spirit was born; the spirit shall cease to be never; never was a time it was not. . . . Birthless and deathless and changeless remaineth the spirit forever."[3] In other words, a person's spirit is eternal, never born and never to die, making afterlife an assumed belief in Hinduism.

Judaism

In general, Judaism is less preoccupied with the afterlife than the other Abrahamic, monotheistic religions (Christianity and Islam). "Nevertheless, there can be no question that classic Judaism had a strong expectation—disorganized, but strong just the same—that certain events will await us all after we die."[4] In the Jewish Torah (first five books of the Old Testament), a good person's death resulted in a reunion with Jewish ancestors like Abraham, Isaac, and Jacob (Genesis 25:8, 17; 49:33; Deuteronomy 32:50). Later in Jewish history, according to the Old Testament book of Daniel, the afterlife bears a resemblance to those of other primary Western religions. Though it's less clearly articulated or emphasized, Judaism also believes life does not end with death.

Islam

Belief in the afterlife is paramount in Islam. Muslims believe there are two destinations for the human soul, and eventually the resurrected human body. According to Islam, the day of judgment is when the earth will be destroyed and everyone will be raised from the dead to be judged by Allah according to their deeds. Once judged, deceased souls will be reunited with their restored bodies to spend eternity in paradise (heaven) or hell. Until the resurrection of the dead, souls are at rest, receiving a foretaste of their eternal destination.

QUESTIONS FOR REFLECTION AND DISCUSSION

- Do you have friends or family who practice a religion other than yours? Have you ever talked with them about their beliefs about the afterlife? What did you learn?

- How might the fact that the vast majority of people believe in life after death point to its reality? How might it not?
- Have you ever been in a situation like Erin's (from the chapter introduction), with a loved one on the brink of death? What did you hope they experienced after dying? Why?

Belief in the afterlife, though it takes different forms, courses through the world's major belief systems. If you performed a one-question "man on the street" interview in Dubai, Shanghai, Tel Aviv, Bangalore, Tehran, or Dallas, much more often than not the response to "Do you believe there is life after death?" would be yes. Given the vast array of cultures, religions, and values represented in each of these far-flung cities, the uniform acknowledgment of an unprovable afterlife is fascinating.

What Does Science Say?

In our book *Answering the Toughest Questions About God and the Bible*, one question we wrestled with was "Why doesn't God make himself more obvious?" Great question, right? While writing that chapter, we met Jacob, a church visitor who struggled with faith. He said, "I've prayed many times for God—if he's out there—to prove it to me."

Jacob's request for God to provide rock-solid proof of his existence reveals the heart of our cultural expectation of God (and everything else, for that matter). In our age of science we rely, more than ever, on measurable, repeatable, physical attributes to "prove" what is real. Miracles are becoming the stuff of legend. If it's real, we want to be able to see, touch, taste, hear, and smell it, or at least confirm it through scientific measurement (because *nobody* has seen or smelled a quark!).

This desire is not new. Thomas, one of Jesus' first devoted followers, wanted the same thing we want: physical proof. When the other disciples claimed Jesus had risen from the dead, he said, "I won't believe it unless I see the nail wounds in his hands, put my fingers in to them, and place my hand into the wound in his side" (John 20:25 NLT).

Since Thomas made that statement two thousand years ago, we've developed tools that are much more powerful than human sight and touch, but our instinctual craving is still like his. When truth claims are made, we say, "Prove it." The same goes for the afterlife.

Humanity has only just begun to lean on science as the one-stop shop for truth (much to the dismay of the faithful who believe there is truth that science cannot measure or prove), but the question is still worth asking. Can science teach us anything about the possibility of the afterlife? And if so, what? Let's jump into a couple of scientific disciplines and see if, and how, they might point toward life after death.

Biology and the afterlife

Every kid has an aha moment. It may come in a conversation with a parent, in a first science class, or upon inspecting fresh roadkill. It's the moment one realizes there is stuff on the inside of us that makes the outside work: hearts in our chests, muscles in our legs, and brains in our heads. But as school-age kids learn more about the facts of physical bodies in biology class, they are also uncovering feelings and thoughts that are far more difficult to assess. How does a junior high girl measure jealousy? How does a boy prove his desire to fit in? How does either measure their developing identity, feelings of love, or burgeoning spiritual intuition? How do we—at any age—explain our self-awareness? The reality is we can't.

The qualities of the body and mind are different. We can measure the literal size of the brain and heart and gauge their physical limits, yet it is impossible to weigh a mind or soul or comprehend its limits. Minds and souls are immaterial, not made of matter like our bodies. In his book *Life After Death: The Evidence,* scholar and Christian apologist Dinesh D'Souza writes:

> The best evidence of contemporary neuroscience is that the mind cannot be equated with the brain, and while deterioration of the brain might impede the operation of the mind, the two are separate, which makes it possible that our immaterial minds and consciousness might survive the termination of our physical frames.[5]

Death of our bodies and brains might not mean death of our minds. What, then, might that say about the potential of life outside, and after, our bodies?

Consciousness

Consciousness is a fascinating thing. It can be turned completely off without the body missing a beat. Conversely, our bodies can be virtually shut down while our consciousness rolls on. Far too many college students (and other adults for that matter) are intimately aware of this. After getting blackout drunk, they may have no conscious recollection of the night before, but their bodies worked just fine. In hospitals everywhere patients under anesthesia are anything but conscious while their hearts keep on ticking. Other patients experience the opposite; they have been paralyzed physically, but their minds are as sharp as ever, painfully conscious of their physical limitation and all that happens around them.

One characteristic of consciousness is clear, and it creates an important question for us. Again, D'Souza explains that consciousness "operates outside the recognized physical laws of nature. One of those laws is, of course, mortality for all living bodies." Then he makes a point that is particularly salient for our topic: "But consciousness is not part of the body."[6] So then does our knowledge (or lack thereof) about consciousness actually show that consciousness after death is possible?

Teleology

Where Biology Lane and Philosophy Street intersect, we discover teleology. If biology is the study of the way things are, teleology is the study of *why* things are. Teleology wrestles not with the origin of species but with the purpose, plan, and trajectory of them. Many people, however, claim the world is void of purpose. The universe sprang into existence at the Big Bang, has expanded ever since, and by evolutionary mishap we've landed at the top of the food chain. Congruent with a belief that the beginning had no meaning is the idea that the end is meaningless, too. When we die, we die. Kaput. No mas. Finito. That's it.

But what if a close examination of evolution revealed a plan behind it? For this idea we need to lean on some heavy hitters. Nobel Prize–winning cellular biologist Christan de Duve puts it like this: "Biological history [has proceeded] through successive ages, from the 'age of chemistry' to the 'age of information' to the 'age of the single cell' to the 'age of multicellular organisms' and finally the 'age of the mind.'"[7] Similarly, Freeman Dyson, a theoretical physicist, writes that what we see in organic life itself is a remarkable progression: "What we see . . . is the universe growing more ordered and more lively as it grows older."[8]

Even though they attribute the cause to evolutionary progress, scientists like de Duve and Dyson believe the mind has developed in a way that's independent of the body. If that's the case, could biology always have pointed, moved, and advanced toward life beyond the biological body itself? Does this make room for life after death?

In Dinesh D'Souza's compelling book, he paints the biological argument for the possibility of an afterlife in a concise stroke. In it we see that the scientific discovery of nature's natural progression points to the possibility of life after death.

> The teleology is the progression, neither random nor accidental in its overall direction, from the simple to the complex, and from physical matter to non-physical mind. . . . Just as nature is part

19

material and perishable, and part immaterial and imperishable, so are we. And it is possible that . . . we, like nature, might have a built-in progression from physical substance to non-physical ideas, from perishable matter to imperishable mind. The time will come when our bodies will irretrievably break down, but it is possible, indeed suggested within the script of nature, that a part of us might outlast these mortal coils.[9]

Scientific proof for life beyond this one? Not quite. But a scientifically viable door that opens the possibility of it? Seems like it to us. And that's quite intriguing.

Physics

If you ever want to have your mind blown, start reading about developments in physics. This, to us, is an unbelievably dynamic branch of science. Without fully opening a subject that is worthy of its own book, we want to pose a few questions as a way of seeing if physics holds open the door for the potential of life after death. Read each and wrestle with the possibilities found in them.

- Physicists are discovering that the universe does not operate in only three dimensions. If other dimensions are possible, could it be that life after death takes place in another dimension?
- Physicists are proving that time, space, and other physical laws of our world do not hold true in other universes. If the rules we live under don't at all apply in other places, could it be that an afterlife—indeed a heaven and hell—is possible?
- Some physicists posit that there are alternate universes (potentially an infinite number of them!). If this hypothesis is true, what else might be true that we can't yet even imagine? Life after death, perhaps?

Even a cursory glance into the study of physics shows that the more we learn, the less we actually know! Physics is opening more doors to more possibilities, not less. A leading figure in quantum physics, Niels Bohr, sometimes told his students that "the problem with your idea is not that it is crazy, but that it is not crazy enough."[10] Bohr's point is ours: Reality can be stranger than science fiction and more bizarre than our wildest imagination. And that might mean life after death is scientifically possible.

QUESTIONS FOR REFLECTION AND DISCUSSION

- Have you ever thought about our knowledge of the afterlife from a scientific perspective? Why or why not?
- Which of the above concepts from science interests you most? Why?
- When you think of science, do you think of it as a discipline that opposes faith or works in partnership with faith? Can you give an example of how science and faith agree (even if scientists and Christians do not!)?

What Do Our Hearts Say?

We don't know about you, but all this is heady stuff for us. And though we are definitely advocates for the regular and proper use of our minds (we give our brains the weekend off), we are happy to say we are people of the heart, as well. There's the stuff you can study, read, and rely on the experts for. But there is also that which can simply be observed, felt, and recognized at the heart of who we are. Here we make two observations that we believe point to the reality of life after death. One is a cultural obsession and the other is a natural desire.

Cultural obsession

Popular legend holds that Ponce de León, the sixteenth-century Spanish conquistador who discovered Florida, was really in search of the ever-elusive fountain of youth. But stories of man's search for magical healing waters are also linked to others throughout time, like Alexander the Great, mythical kings of the Middle Ages, and elixir salesmen in the Wild West. Similar fairy tales are found in far-flung places like the Canary Islands, Japan, Polynesia, and England.[11] And though we may roll our educated eyes at the idea of mystical, miracle-working waters, our actions prove that we are still on the hunt for a cure for our ever-aging bodies.

There's proof of this pursuit all around us. Here's a short list that lays bare our obsession with defeating death:

- *Medicine*—The most obvious "fountain of youth" is our ever-increasing medical advancement. This, by the way, is *very good*! We *should* be interested in healing diseases and fixing bodies. But our feverish attempts to medically extend life reveal our deep desire to live forever.

- *Age-defying products*—Have you noticed the plethora of skin-care and makeup products available at your local drug store and in TV commercials? Each wrinkle-reducing cream and age-defying makeup promises to hide every sign of aging.

- *Plastic surgery*—We live in Southern California, the plastic surgery capital of the world. Our culture's obsession with youth has spawned a multibillion-dollar cosmetic surgery industry.

- *Emphasis on the young*—Our movie screens, television sets, and tabloid magazines are constantly plastered with pictures of the young and beautiful. The celebrity faces that sell the latest "Wrinkle-Be-Gone" lotion aren't even old enough to have wrinkles. Hollywood projects the not-so-subtle message that "Once you're over thirty, you're old," and then it asks, "Don't you wish you were young and beautiful again?"

- *Forgetting the old*—Our obsession with youth creates the sad reality that our elderly, much more so than in many other societies, are all but forgotten and left to die alone in nursing homes with others who have aged out of our social consciousness. Hopefully, if we can hide the dying, we can forget we are one of them.

So what does our obsession with medicine and youth have to do with the afterlife? Aren't these cultural obsessions simply ways to encourage and celebrate health, wellness, and beauty? On the surface, the answer is yes. But our fixation on youth and dodging death is not simply because we want to live well, but because we all desire to live forever.

Natural desire

C. S. Lewis, the twentieth-century Christian theologian, professor, and author, believed our deep-seated desire for the afterlife was a powerful argument for its existence. His logic went something like this:

1. Every natural innate desire has a real object that can fulfill it.
2. Human beings have a natural innate desire for immortality.
3. Therefore, there must be immortal life after death.

Norman Geisler says it this way: "It is argued that if there is hunger there is food; if thirst, drink; if *eros*, sexual fulfillment; if curiosity, knowledge; and if loneliness, society."[12] Interestingly, our desire for the afterlife, unlike the desires above, is for something that cannot be proved and is not easily defined (thus the reason for this book). Yet all of humanity for all of history has longed for a future life. Doesn't the desire, then, point to one? Geisler continues by writing, "If these premises are true, there is 'more' to this life. . . . We may never attain it, but this no more disproves its existence than . . . starvation proves there is no food anywhere."[13]

In this life we crave things because there is a very real satisfaction for it. Is life after death one of those very real things?

QUESTIONS FOR REFLECTION AND DISCUSSION

- What do you think is the most compelling, nonreligious clue for the afterlife?

- If you are not religious, what do you think about the reality of life after death? Do science and our natural inclinations point toward it? Why or why not?
- If you are religious, how does this conversation about life after death inform or shape your beliefs about it?
- Does your heart long for the afterlife? Does your life show that you believe in the afterlife even if you are unsure of it intellectually? In what ways?

What Does Christianity Say?

As we mentioned at the very beginning of this chapter, Christians give a resounding yes when asked if they believe in life after death. But where do Christians get information about heaven, hell, and the afterlife? We're certain you can answer this question without us, but since we're writing a book about it, we feel obliged to type it out: The answer is the Bible. But what are some key portions of the Bible in regard to the afterlife? We're glad you asked.

The linchpin

In 1 Corinthians 15, the apostle Paul (who penned a substantial chunk of the New Testament) wrote some pretty strong words about Jesus, his followers, and the resurrection of the dead.

If Christ has not been raised [from the dead], then all our preaching is useless, and your faith is useless. And we apostles would all be lying about God—for we have said that God raised Christ from the grave. But that can't be true if there is no resurrection of the dead. And if there is no resurrection of the dead, then Christ has not been raised. And if Christ has not been raised, then your faith is useless and you are still guilty of your sins. In that case, all who have died believing in Christ are lost! And if our hope in Christ is only for this life, we are more to be pitied than anyone in the world.

1 Corinthians 15:14–19 NLT

Paul knew that the crucial fact for knowing if there is life after death is whether or not Jesus of Nazareth actually rose from the grave. Though many non-Christians argue against it, the historical evidence for the resurrection is reliable. For Christians, Paul could not be more correct. Jesus' death and resurrection is the linchpin of Christian belief. Everything hinges on that, and it is the primary way Christians know eternal life is possible. Without that historical event, the reality of life after death is but a guessing game. But because it happened, Jesus' teachings about the afterlife can be trusted. The following gives us a glimpse into those teachings.

Life after death in the Bible

It's probably no surprise that the most prolific voice in Scripture about life after death was Jesus. He rose from the grave and raised others from death. But did he believe it possible for *all* his followers? Here is how the writers of the Gospels (the four biographical books in the Bible about Jesus) recorded Jesus' words about life after death in regard to us.

In a conversation about spirituality with Nicodemus, a prominent Jewish religious leader, Jesus delivered one of the most famous lines in all of history. It includes his divine understanding of the afterlife. Jesus said,

"For God so loved the world that he gave his one and only Son, that whoever believes in him shall not perish but have eternal life."

John 3:16

When Jesus was put to death by crucifixion, a criminal suffering the same fate said to Jesus, "Remember me when you come into your kingdom" (Luke 23:42). Jesus' answer affirms heaven: "Truly I tell you, today you will be with me in paradise" (verse 43).

Jesus once initiated a remarkable turn of events that displayed his power over death. After his dear friend Lazarus died, Jesus said to Lazarus' grieving sister, "I am the resurrection and the life. The one who believes in me will live, even though they die; and whoever lives by believing in me will never die" (John 11:25–26). Then Jesus strode into his dead friend's tomb, prayed to God, and commanded Lazarus to "come out!" (John 11:43). The once very much dead Lazarus immediately became very much alive.

More Than Possible

Is there life after death? Most of humanity believes there is. Science keeps that possibility alive. Our hearts long for it. Our actions confirm we believe it. And to top it off, Christians worship a God-man who actually died and rose again, helped others live past death, and promises we will, too.

Christianity is based on the life, death, resurrection, ascension, and promised return of Jesus. Christianity, without doubt, teaches that we are eternal beings. We are destined, one way or the other, to live on past this earthly life. Jesus, we believe, is the proof of and the provision for life after death. The questions that now unfold before us are about the specific nature of that postdeath life. Hang on to your hat, because the journey through death and the life thereafter is going to be quite the trip.

QUESTIONS FOR REFLECTION AND DISCUSSION

- How does Jesus' resurrection impact the truth of an afterlife for you?
- Why would Paul say Christians are fools if Christ did not rise from the dead?
- What did you believe about the afterlife before you read this chapter? What do you believe about it now? Why are they different or the same?
- If the afterlife is indeed real, what is your greatest remaining question about it?

2

What Happens When You Die?

Introduction

When I (Stan) got the call from a friend I had not seen for a couple of years, I was happy to hear his voice. We small-talked for a few minutes, catching up on each other's lives, before he told me something I never expected. Not in a million years. "I have stage 4 cancer." He said it with little emotion and continued speaking as my mouth dropped open. I was grateful he couldn't see my facial expression. "The doctors tell me I have a 5 percent chance of survival." My reaction: more jaw dropping. I couldn't think of what to say, so I stumbled on my words and just listened.

As my friend told me more, his life flashed before my eyes—I saw his wife and his children, his business and his house—and at the end of my mental review, I saw him dying. I know, that's a terrible thing to ponder about someone, but I couldn't help it. I felt such despair, and a profound sadness came over me. I did my best to express empathy while I listened, and then I finally muttered what must have sounded like trite encouragement. I'm not sure how helpful I was, and it bothered me that I didn't have anything profound to offer.

In the last chapter we showed that belief in the afterlife is almost universal. All the major religions emphasize it in one way or another. Scientists, in an attempt to explain why the mind is developing apart from the body, have left the door open for life after death. And those who believe the Christian story understand that the linchpin for belief in a literal hereafter is the life, death, resurrection, ascension, and promised return of Jesus.

Despite all of these positive signs pointing to life after death, there's one part of this reality that's difficult if not impossible for us to deal with, and that's death itself. Let's admit it. We all love the idea of life going on forever, but nobody wants to die. In fact, if it were up to us, we would skip the dying part and go straight to what's on the other side—hoping against hope that it's heaven rather than hell.

But there's no way to get there without facing the Grim Reaper. So let's talk about death. We admit it's not a cheery subject, but we have to face it sometime, so we might as well get death out in the open.

We could open our discussion with a simple statement like "Death is everywhere," but that would seem a little morbid. Come to think of it, any discussion about death is inherently morbid, so let's not let that stop us. Let's face the fact that death is one of the most common occurrences on the planet. According to the National Center for Health Statistics, more than 7,000 people die each day in the U.S.[1] Nearly 11,000 are born each day,[2] so there's reason for hope: Babies outnumber corpses. Yet death is a very present reality, reminding us that every baby eventually dies. The Bible puts it rather matter-of-factly: "People are destined to die once" (Hebrews 9:27).

Getting Angry at Death

Despite its ubiquity, we don't think much about death until it becomes something personal, like getting a phone call from a friend or learning that an elderly family member hasn't got long to live. Or hearing from a doctor that you have an incurable disease.

28

That kind of news, no matter where it comes from or whom it's about, is devastating. We hate it. So our initial inclination is to deny it's true, and when reality sets in, we get angry and feel the urge to fight back. Call it chutzpah or arrogance or simply the will to survive and live, we don't take death lying down. Especially in the U.S., there is a growing reluctance to give in to the Grim Reaper. In 1990, 15 percent of all U.S. adults said doctors should do everything possible to keep a patient alive, even when confronted with an incurable illness. Today, twice as many people hold that view.

Two-thirds of U.S. adults agree there are circumstances when a patient should be allowed to die,[3] but the number of people who would advocate for aggressive treatment in the face of overwhelming odds is growing.

Some people (and by "some people" we mean very rich people) are pouring millions of dollars into longevity research. Google CEO Larry Page has launched an initiative that will attempt to "significantly expand human lifespan."[4] PayPal co-founder Peter Thiel wants to live to 120 and is doing everything he can to make that happen, from investing in longevity research to radically altering his diet.[5] Oracle founder Larry Ellison created The Ellison Medical Foundation to support aging research. "Death makes me angry,"[6] the eccentric billionaire said.

Before criticizing these rich guys for their death avoidance, we'd like to suggest that anger at death is an entirely appropriate response.

QUESTIONS FOR REFLECTION AND DISCUSSION

- What is your view on doing what it takes to prolong life?
- Why do you think it's so hard for us to give in to death?
- As you have observed the way people respond in the face of death, do you think Christians react any differently than non-Christians do?
- Have Christians made an idol of life? If you think so, in what way has this happened?

Jesus Confronts Death

There is a dramatic story in the eleventh chapter of the Gospel of John about Jesus and a friend and death. To put the story in context, Jesus has just made a public announcement that he is the Good Shepherd of God's sheep (John 10:1–21). While that doesn't sound all that controversial, it's a bold claim to the religious leaders. They immediately equate his words with Psalm 23, where God is portrayed as the shepherd. In effect, Jesus is claiming to be the same as God. Jesus spells it out for anyone who doesn't make the shepherd connection:

> "My sheep listen to my voice; I know them, and they follow me. I give them eternal life, and they shall never perish; no one will snatch them out of my hand. My Father, who has given them to me, is greater than all; no one can snatch them out of my Father's hand. I and the Father are one."
>
> John 10:27–30

It's one thing for Jesus to make the claim that he is one with God and qualified to give eternal life, and quite another to prove it. And that's precisely what Jesus does when he is brought face-to-face with the death of his good friend Lazarus.

On one level, the account of Jesus and the death of Lazarus is a very human story. Lazarus and his sisters are real people Jesus loves and cares about. This story also operates on a superhuman level that very much goes to the center of this book. If there truly is such a thing as eternal life with God in heaven, what happens in this story is a major component of that reality. Jesus has just said he will give his sheep eternal life, and now he is going to make good on that promise. But not before he confronts death head on.

Because he's Jesus, he doesn't do things the way we would. If we were informed that a friend was at death's door, we'd be there in a heartbeat. Not Jesus. He takes his time, so much time that Lazarus dies, and by the time Jesus finally does arrive, he's been dead for four days (John 11:17). No doubt the family was glad to see Jesus, but clearly they were disappointed. "If you had been here," they tell him, "our brother would not have died."

Jesus Is Life

Jesus is not indifferent. He understands what is happening. He looks at them and says those immortal words that are repeated countless times at Christian funerals around the world. We urge you to read these words as one who is living and can look forward to eternal life because of the power and promise of Jesus:

> "I am the resurrection and the life. The one who believes in me will live, even though they die; and whoever lives by believing in me will never die. Do you believe this?"
>
> John 11:25–26

Those words should be enough for the family of Lazarus. They should be enough for us. But there's more! Jesus doesn't just *say* he gives eternal life. He gives a demonstration. But not before he gets angry at death. As Jesus nears the tomb where Lazarus' dead body lies, he observes the family weeping. And he loses it. Some have argued that Jesus became angry at the unbelief of those around him. But the context and the description say otherwise. Jesus was angry at death and its grim, horrible grip on humankind. And Jesus wept (John 11:35).

Jesus Hates Death, so He Killed It

Others around Jesus are weeping, too, but their tears of grief are for the loss of a friend and brother. Jesus' tears are tears of rage, caused by the tyranny of Satan, sin, and death.

We don't just have a Savior and an Advocate who is unhappy with the mortality all of us face. He hates it so much that he was willing to go toe-to-toe with Satan and head-to-head with death by dying himself and then rising from the dead, thereby crushing Satan and defeating death forever.

Jesus raised Lazarus from the dead simply by speaking his name. You can only imagine the shock and the joy that followed. The grave had no choice but to give up Lazarus. Death stood no chance against the one who overcomes death and gives eternal life. And what was true for Lazarus then is true for us today. Jesus loves us and Jesus hates death. Therefore, anyone who believes in him will not die but have eternal life.

We shouldn't be surprised at Jesus' response to death, although we may be perplexed that he reacted so emotionally. After all, wasn't death part of the reason Jesus was sent to earth in the first place? When the Bible says in its most famous verse, "For God so loved the world that he gave his one and only Son," we know that God's "giving" Jesus meant that God sent Jesus into the world to die. That's a critical part of the story. Jesus had to experience death personally in order for sinners to be saved.

> For if, while we were God's enemies, we were reconciled to him through the death of his Son, how much more, having been reconciled, shall we be saved through his life!
>
> Romans 5:10

But there's more to the story than that. It doesn't stop with the death of Jesus. As we have already pointed out (and will likely emphasize a few more times before this book is finished), the gospel message of the Bible—the good news for the entire world—is that death doesn't have to be the end game. By his own death and resurrection, Jesus conquered death for us. To put it more graphically, he killed death. He died and rose from the dead to show us it could be done, to demonstrate that death has been defeated. The apostle Paul puts it this way: "For we know that since Christ was raised from the dead, he cannot die again; death no longer has mastery over him" (Romans 6:9). And since death no longer has mastery over Jesus, it no longer has mastery over those who put their faith in him.

QUESTIONS FOR REFLECTION AND DISCUSSION

- Describe what it feels like to know that Jesus hates death even more than you do.
- In what way is Satan responsible for death? What does that mean to you today?
- How are Satan, sin, and death related? What does each one have to do with the other two?

Death May Not Sting, but It Still Hurts

But death is still with us. Those who believe in Jesus die, and those who don't believe die. There doesn't seem to be any difference. Death does not discriminate. Christian or not, old or young, rich or poor, everyone dies. Yet as despicable as death is, the Bible tells us we don't need to fear it. In the most famous in-your-face statement against death found in the Bible, the apostle Paul writes,

"Death has been has been swallowed up in victory."
"Where, O death, is your victory? Where, O death, is your sting?"

1 Corinthians 15:54–55

Talk about chutzpah! And yet, does bravado like that have meaning for someone who's actually facing death? How does saying "Death has been swallowed up in victory" help someone face death with dignity and assurance? How do the words give comfort to someone who's actually dying? In our experience, we don't think they do, at least not when someone is in the throes of fighting death.

After Stan learned that his friend had stage 4 cancer, he starting meeting with him. The first couple of meetings were one-way conversations, with Stan's friend describing what he was going through. He was as positive as one could be in his situation. He talked mostly about the medical treatments being employed to combat and hopefully defeat his disease. At the third meeting Stan told his friend he was writing a book about heaven and hell.

33

Without missing a beat, Stan's friend said, "I don't think much about heaven. I'm concentrating on surviving here on earth."

There's no question Stan's friend believes in heaven, so it's not that he views heaven as some sort of fairy tale. He's just a little preoccupied with staying alive. His earthly existence, which had been pretty darn good, is right here in front of him, while heaven seems so far away. From his experience, life is definitely worth fighting for.

And there's one more dynamic that reinforces his will to live: he doesn't want to die. And is that such a bad thing? Is his attitude any different from Larry Page's, Peter Thiel's, or Larry Ellison's? They don't want to die any more than Stan's friend wants to die. And neither do you. None of us wants to die.

Nobody Wants to Die

The legendary country singer Loretta Lynn spoke for all of us when she wrote, "Everybody wants to go to heaven, but nobody wants to die." Leave it to a coal miner's daughter to express in simple words what we all feel about death. We hate it. Consequently, we do everything we can to avoid it, to not think about it, or to otherwise defeat it, if only for a few years. The trouble is, no one except Jesus has ever defeated death, no one has ever escaped death, and no one ever will. So it doesn't do any good to avoid it. We need to at the very least try to understand death.

Maybe the reason none of us want to die and few of us are looking forward to heaven is that we don't know what happens when we die. We have good questions:

- Do we simply cease to exist?
- Will we float on clouds in a spirit-life existence?
- Will be become angels?
- Will we have some kind of disembodied experience?

But we rarely if ever get satisfying answers. So we put heaven out of our minds (because you have to die to get there) and focus on earth.

God Wants Us to Know

The truth is, God wants us to know about death and even look forward to it—not the dying part, but the life that follows. And he has given us enough information (call them clues) to tell us the sequence of events triggered by death. These are found in the Bible, which is by all measurements the most reliable source of information about all of life and death and the afterlife.

How can we be so sure about that? For one thing, we trust the Bible. In fact, our book *Answering the Toughest Questions About God and the Bible* responded to questions about the reliability of God's Word. Without going into detail here (we're hoping you add that title to your list of books to read), we will say this: The Bible has been shown through history, scholarship, and experience to be utterly faithful in all it says about God and the human condition.

And here's something to consider when it comes to predicting the future, including yours. The Bible includes statements about future events. In fact, there are more than 2,500 prophecies in the Bible. Approximately 80 percent of these have been fulfilled to the letter, including hundreds of historically demonstrable prophecies fulfilled in the life, death, and resurrection of Jesus Christ. The remaining 20 percent concern events that haven't yet occurred. Because the Bible's track record for accuracy is 100 percent, the odds of those unfulfilled events coming to pass the way the Bible describes—even if we don't fully understand what they mean—are pretty good. Astronomically good.

So it's not unreasonable to dig in to the Bible and see if there are any statements or descriptions about what will happen when we die.

QUESTIONS FOR REFLECTION AND DISCUSSION

- Does 1 Corinthians 15:54–55 give you any comfort or confidence? Why or why not?
- Explain how it is possible to believe in heaven but not have a desire to go there, even if you're facing a potentially deadly situation.

> • We listed four questions people have about death. What are
> some of your questions?

Seven Things the Bible Says About Death

Besides the eternal truth that death has been swallowed up in victory, here are seven biblical truths about death for the Christian:

1. *The moment after death, you will immediately be in the presence of Jesus.* This reality comes to us directly from Jesus, who promises the thief who is being crucified next to him, "Truly I tell you, today you will be with me in paradise" (Luke 23:43). In his letter to the Philippian church, written from prison, the apostle Paul states this often-quoted phrase: "For to me, to live is Christ and to die is gain" (Philippians 1:21). In fact, he is torn between the desire to "depart and be with Christ" and the necessity of remaining with the believers (verses 23–24).

   This is not the final, eternal state but is rather the "intermediate" state. As we will see in chapter 9, heaven is a real place where God dwells, and at some point in the future, all those who have trusted Jesus by faith will dwell with him and all the believers throughout human history in the new heaven and the new earth in their resurrected bodies. But immediately upon death, all believers go into the presence of Jesus.

   The phrase *intermediate state* is a theological term used to describe the time between a believer's death and the return of Christ, also known as the second coming. Paul describes this world-changing event in a letter to the Thessalonian church, which is growing despite persecution. His purpose in the letter is to encourage the believers in their trials and to give them a glimpse into the future. Notice in this passage how Paul distinguishes between those believers who die before Christ returns and those who are "still alive":

Brothers and sisters, we do not want you to be uninformed about those who sleep in death, so that you do not grieve like the rest of mankind, who have no hope. For we believe that Jesus died and rose again, and so we believe that God will bring with Jesus those who have fallen asleep in him. According to the Lord's word, we tell you that we who are still alive, who are left until the coming of the Lord, will certainly not precede those who have fallen asleep. For the Lord himself will come down from heaven, with a loud command, with the voice of the archangel and with the trumpet call of God, and the dead in Christ will rise first. After that, we who are still alive and are left will be caught up together with them in the clouds to meet the Lord in the air. And so we will be with the Lord forever. Therefore encourage one another with these words.

1 Thessalonians 4:13–18

2. *When you die, there will be inexpressible joy.* According to the Psalms, to be in the presence of Jesus is to experience joy:

You make known to me the path of life; you fill me with joy in your presence, with eternal pleasures at your right hand.

Psalm 16:11

3. *After you die, there will be no more pain.* We often say of someone who has died after battling a terrible illness, "Thank God they aren't suffering anymore." It may sound trite at the time (and we don't recommend saying it out loud), but it's absolutely true. Being in the presence of Jesus means there is no more pain or sorrow or death.

4. *You will eventually have a new body.* Your body, no matter what the condition, will be made completely new. Think of it as a total body makeover, only without dieting and exercise. As we said, it won't happen immediately upon your death, but when Jesus returns to earth at his second coming. For

those who have died, Paul makes a distinction between the "perishable" body and the "imperishable" body:

> So it will be with the resurrection of the dead. The body that is sown is perishable, it is raised imperishable; it is sown in dishonor, it is raised in glory; it is sown in weakness, it is raised in power; it is sown a natural body, it is raised a spiritual body.
>
> 1 Corinthians 15:42–44

5. *When you die, you will not face punishment.* There is *judgment*, but there is no punishment for the believer who dies. The Bible says, "Therefore, there is now no condemnation for those who are in Christ Jesus" (Romans 8:1). We can't overestimate how powerful this truth is. No matter what we have done, if we have asked for and accepted God's forgiveness made possible through Christ Jesus, we are not condemned.

So what about judgment for believers? It takes place after the return of Christ, and it's a final judgment for believers and nonbelievers alike (Matthew 10:15; 11:22, 24; Acts 17:30–31; Revelation 20:11–15). Those who have not put their trust in Christ will be judged according to their works (Romans 2:5–8; Revelation 20:12–13). Believers will appear before the judgment seat of Christ, "so that each of us may receive what is due us for the things done while in the body, whether good or bad" (2 Corinthians 5:10).

6. *You will not miss what you had on earth.* Despite the pain and sorrow of this world, it's still a pretty nice place to live. And no matter how rough you've had it in life, there will be things you will miss. At least that's what you think now. In truth, you will not miss what you had on earth—whether relationships or stuff you're fond of—because your perspective on what is important will be changed. "For now we see only a reflection as in a mirror" (1 Corinthians 13:12a). As C. S. Lewis says, we live in the shadowlands. As much as we'd

like to think we see all of reality now, we see only reflections. We see only shadows. When we are in the presence of Jesus, we will see face-to-face. We will know fully, even as we are fully known (1 Corinthians 13:12b).

7. *You will be missed on earth, but your family and friends will be happy for you.* Or to be more specific, your family and friends who believe in Jesus the way you do will be happy for you. They will be sorrowful, but they will have the confidence that you are in the presence of Jesus.

Eternity Starts Now

As Stan began meeting with his friend after hearing the news of his stage 4 cancer, he began to formulate a narrative that would offer encouragement. There's no sugarcoating death, he told his friend. It's the worst life has to offer—a tragic and cruel event that haunts us while we live, toys with us as we grow older, and sometimes stabs us in the back when we least expect it. We can take some comfort in knowing that God hates death more than we do, but ultimately our hope is found in the life, death, and resurrection of Jesus, who destroyed death so that we may live.

That's good news indeed, but there's even better news. We don't have to wait until we're dead to experience this life God offers through his Son. For everyone who trusts in Jesus for salvation, eternity starts now.

> But because of his great love for us, God, who is rich in mercy, made us alive with Christ even when we were dead in transgressions—it is by grace you have been saved. And God raised us up with Christ and seated us with him in the heavenly realms in Christ Jesus, in order that in the coming ages he might show the incomparable riches of his grace, expressed in his kindness to us in Christ Jesus.
>
> Ephesians 2:4–7

Yes, death is a reality and it sucks, but from the perspective of eternity, death is merely a transition from this life, where we "see only a reflection as in a mirror." On the other side of death, a transition that will transpire in the twinkling of an eye, we will fully know, even as we are fully known.

Life after death isn't a myth or a fairy tale. It's real. That's what Stan said to his friend, and that's what we're telling you. When you die, there will be sadness for those still living, but not for you who believe. Only inexpressible joy and infinite wonder at the life you will then have.

QUESTIONS FOR REFLECTION AND DISCUSSION

- Of the seven things listed that the Bible says about death, list the three that are most compelling to you. Explain why those three.
- What's the difference between judgment and punishment?
- How does your perspective about life and death change when you understand that death is merely a transition from this life to the next?

3

Are Heaven and Hell
for Real?

Introduction

Rebecca is a biologist. She spends her days staring into microscopes to watch how cancer cells multiply and grow. Her perspective on the world is deeply rooted in the scientifically provable. If it can't be seen and studied, then it's not for her. Yet ironically, she can't help but read every book about individuals' near-death experiences.

"So you've read all of them?" I asked.

"Oh yeah. I can't get enough of them," she replied enthusiastically. "It's like a train wreck: I don't want to read them, but I can't quite help looking at it all."

"So . . . what do you think—as a scientist—about people's claims to have been to heaven and back?"

"I think it's true. The people have definitely been somewhere. But not physically," she said. "The mind is a powerful thing! And when I read those books, a person's mind is what I'm getting a glimpse into, not heaven or hell. And I think it's fascinating!"

Then she turned the questions to me. "Haven't you gone places in your mind that you can't prove? Haven't you imagined you've visited places that aren't real?"

"Of course!" I laughed. I could not deny it. Like everyone, I had ventured to places intellectually that I have never been and cannot prove exist, physically.

"So let me ask you, then," Rebecca said after a pause, "are heaven and hell for real? I sure haven't seen the science—no golden dirt and nobody with burn marks."

■ ■ ■

This is a fair and appropriate question, and certainly a legitimate inquiry for anyone who is evaluating the claims of Jesus Christ. Of course, many people over the last two thousand years have already formulated an answer to this question (even before reading this chapter, imagine that), including

- the billions of people who have "accepted Jesus" with the expectation that they are going to spend eternity with him;
- the billions of people who have believed in religions other than Christianity that have a different postdeath reality (such as reincarnation in Hinduism and Buddhism); and
- the billions of people who lived with no regard to an afterlife because they assumed there wasn't one, or that they would simply "take their chances."

But even if you fall into one of these already-have-an-answer groups, we suspect you'll be interested if we present clear-cut, incontrovertible, scientific proof for the definitive answer. But you know we can't. This question probes the spiritual realm, outside the confines of our dimensions of time and space. We can't "prove" heaven and hell by pointing to them on some galactic map. Conversely, the reality of heaven and hell cannot be *disproved* simply because we don't see them.

QUESTIONS FOR REFLECTION AND DISCUSSION

- Is Rebecca correct? Can we abandon science as the ultimate (and exclusive) form of proof?
- Do you think heaven and hell are real?
- If you do, then what type of proof have you relied upon to support your belief? If not, then what type of proof would you require before you could change your present opinion?

Jesus Talked About Heaven and Hell Like They Are Real

While we may be a little skeptical about those bestselling books of someone who has visited heaven for a couple of hours and returned to earth to tell about it, we won't deny that it happened. How could *we* know? We believe it will be more productive, however, if we consider what *Jesus* said about heaven and hell. (For more of our thoughts on near-death experiences, see appendix 4.)

Even if you aren't a Christian, you need to consider Jesus as a source of information on this topic because: (1) he claimed to be the Son of God (John 10:36); (2) he claimed to have descended from heaven to earth (John 6:38); (3) he talked more about hell than any other person in the Bible;[1] and (4) he told his disciples he was going to return to heaven (John 16:28). Who better than Jesus to interview about this subject?

Things Jesus said about heaven

Here are just a few samples of what Jesus said about heaven. As you read these verses, keep this question in mind: "Does it seem that Jesus really believes in the reality of heaven?"

43

- The night before he was crucified, in an effort to comfort his disciples over what was about to happen, Jesus assured them that they would eventually be with him in heaven:

  "Don't let your hearts be troubled. Trust in God, and trust also in me. There is more than enough room in my Father's home. If this were not so, would I have told you that I am going to prepare a place for you? When everything is ready, I will come and get you, so that you will always be with me where I am. And you know the way to where I am going."

  John 14:1–4 NLT

- Jesus always referred to his Father as residing in heaven:

  "Whoever denies me before men, I also will deny before my Father who is in heaven."

  Matthew 10:33 ESV

- Christ taught that salvation involved turning away from your sins as a condition to receiving the reward of heaven:

  [Jesus] said, "I tell you the truth, unless you turn from your sins and become like little children, you will never get into the Kingdom of Heaven."

  Matthew 18:2–3 NLT

Now read those verses again, this time asking yourself, "Does it seem that Jesus really wants his audience to believe in the reality of heaven?"

Things Jesus said about hell

Jesus knew and spoke a lot about hell. Unlike many contemporary preachers (as we'll discuss in chapter 6), Jesus didn't dodge the subject.

- Jesus used the prospect of hell as motivation for people to pursue a lifestyle pleasing to God.

44

"And if your right hand causes you to stumble, cut it off and throw it away. It is better for you to lose one part of your body than for your whole body to go into hell."

Matthew 5:30

- Jesus used descriptions of hell to impress upon his audiences the stark consequences of rejecting his gospel message:

"And I tell you this, that many Gentiles will come from all over the world—from east and west—and sit down with Abraham, Isaac, and Jacob at the feast in the Kingdom of Heaven. But many Israelites—those for whom the Kingdom was prepared—will be thrown into outer darkness, where there will be weeping and gnashing of teeth."

Matthew 8:11–12 NLT

- Jesus continually warned of God's judgment and wrath for those who do not believe and follow him.

"This is how it will be at the end of the age. The angels will come and separate the wicked from the righteous and throw them into the blazing furnace, where there will be weeping and gnashing of teeth."

Matthew 13:49–50

The consequence of hell was a favorite subject of Jesus. He could hardly stop talking about it. Do you think he would make such a big deal about it if hell didn't really exist?

Jesus Often Contrasted Heaven with Hell

Some of Christ's most descriptive references about heaven and hell were made together, as he contrasted one with the other. He was always intent and passionate when making these comparisons, giving equal weight and significance to the diametrically opposed consequences at opposite ends of the eternal life spectrum. The impact of what he says would be greatly diminished if Jesus believed only one of them to be actual and the other to be fictional. What is your assessment? Do the following contrasts between heaven and hell (eternal life versus death) give you insight about Christ's belief in the reality of neither, one, or both?

- Jesus preached a mini-sermon on the subject of God's judgment. In it he revealed the respective eternal destinies when he contrasted the wicked with the righteous:

> "When the Son of Man comes in his glory, and all the angels with him, then he will sit upon his glorious throne. All the nations will be gathered in his presence, and he will separate the people as a shepherd separates the sheep from the goats. He will place the sheep at his right hand and the goats at his left.
>
> "Then the King will say to those on his right, 'Come, you who are blessed by my Father, inherit the Kingdom prepared for you from the creation of the world. For I was hungry, and you fed me. I was thirsty, and you gave me a drink. I was a stranger, and you invited me into your home. I was naked, and you gave me clothing. I was sick, and you cared for me. I was in prison, and you visited me.'
>
> "Then these righteous ones will reply, 'Lord, when did we ever see you hungry and feed you? Or thirsty and give you something to drink? Or a stranger and show you hospitality? Or naked and give you clothing? When did we ever see you sick or in prison and visit you?'
>
> "And the King will say, 'I tell you the truth, when you did it to one of the least of these my brothers and sisters, you were doing it to me!'
>
> "Then the King will turn to those on the left and say, 'Away with you, you cursed ones, into the eternal fire prepared for the devil and his demons. For I was hungry, and you didn't feed me. I was thirsty, and you didn't give me a drink. I was a stranger, and you didn't invite me into your home. I was

naked, and you didn't give me clothing. I was sick and in prison, and you didn't visit me.'

"Then they will reply, 'Lord, when did we ever see you hungry or thirsty or a stranger or naked or sick or in prison, and not help you?'

"And he will answer, 'I tell you the truth, when you refused to help the least of these my brothers and sisters, you were refusing to help me.'

"And they will go away into eternal punishment, but the righteous will go into eternal life."

Matthew 25:31–46 NLT

- Jesus makes another similar contrast, with similar outcomes, when he is confronted by hypocritical religious leaders. As with the previous passage, the following verses refer to the judgment at the end of time. Instead of *heaven* versus *hell*, the code words are *life* versus *judgment*.

"Don't act so surprised at all this. The time is coming when everyone dead and buried will hear his voice. Those who have lived the right way will walk out into a resurrection Life; those who have lived the wrong way, into a resurrection Judgment."

John 5:28–29 THE MESSAGE

The opposing outcomes of heaven and hell always arise when Jesus contrasts those who repent and follow Christ as Lord with those who continue in their sin and reject Christ. At the end of the Sermon on the Mount, Jesus presents this drastic distinction with a metaphor. Again, no "heaven" and "hell" terminology, but the contrast is described as "life" versus "destruction."

"Enter through the narrow gate. For wide is the gate and broad is the road that leads to destruction, and many enter through it. But small is the gate and narrow the road that leads to life, and only a few find it."

Matthew 7:13–14

Dealing with Existential Questions

The existence of heaven and hell isn't the only "How do you prove what you can't see?" question that confronts Christianity. A bigger—and more often asked—question is this: "How can you know that *God* is real?" As this question has been asked over the centuries, several answers have developed, all relying on rational proof. The answers acknowledge that God is a spirit, and no one has seen him, but his existence can be established by logical arguments. Here are four of the most famous such arguments:

1. The ontological argument

This argument, a philosophical one, proposes that the very fact that humans have an idea of God points to his existence. Experts agree that a pursuit of, or belief in, the divine can be found among all peoples and tribes of the earth. Since every rational person has thought about God in one way or another, we can reasonably conclude that he exists. Example: Even if you can't see the moon or explain exactly what the moon is, the tides show the moon's presence. In the same way, humans have always felt a tug toward a Supreme Being. Even though God can't be seen, the incredibly strong pull we feel toward him is an evidence of his existence.

For since the creation of the world God's invisible qualities—his eternal power and divine nature—have been clearly seen, being understood from what has been made, so that men are without excuse.

Romans 1:20

2. The cosmological argument

Every effect must have a cause. A four-year-old might really believe his muddy footprints just happened by themselves, but his mom sure knows differently. If the universe had a beginning point—which science confirms—there must have been some incredibly powerful cause or person to begin it. Science refers to this cause or person as the First Cause. The Bible says it is God.

For every house is built by someone, but God is the builder of everything.

Hebrews 3:4

3. The teleological argument

There is order, harmony, purpose, and intelligence in nature and the world. Logic suggests that an intelligent and purposeful being produced it. If you saw a stunning mansion built on a cliff high above the ocean, you would know that a master architect and skilled builders were involved. Likewise, the amazing and beautiful ocean below and the magnificent nighttime sky above make a strong argument for the existence of an amazing intelligence behind them. (In fact, the more beautiful, complex, and perfectly ordered the creation, the more intelligent and powerful the creator would be.)

The heavens declare the glory of God; the skies proclaim the work of his hands.

Psalm 19:1

4. The moral argument

One of the characteristics of humans is that we have a moral code—a built-in sense of right and wrong. This has been true of every people group and every civilization in recorded history. How could a moral compass—often called the higher law—just happen? The sense of right and wrong in the heart of every person is evidence of a moral Creator.

> Indeed, when Gentiles, who do not have the law, do by nature things required by the law, they are a law for themselves, even though they do not have the law. They show that the requirements of the law are written on their hearts, their consciences also bearing witness, and their thoughts sometimes accusing them and at other times even defending them.
>
> Romans 2:14–15

QUESTIONS FOR REFLECTION AND DISCUSSION

- Although not providing definitive proof, do these arguments move you forward in a belief in the existence and reality of God?
- Do you find one of the arguments more convincing than the others? Why is that?
- Can you apply a similar line of rational arguments to the subject of the reality of heaven and hell? What arguments would you make?

Arguments for the Existence of Heaven and Hell

Just as there are rational arguments for the existence of God, there are several overwhelming, logical arguments for the reality of heaven and hell. We'll present the two that are the most convincing to us. You won't be as impressed with the weight of these arguments if you believe that Jesus was a fraud or a lunatic, some guy who perpetrated a religious scam that has lasted over two thousand years. But if you believe that Jesus is legit, and that he sacrificed his life for the sake of humanity, then we think these arguments may put to rest any questions you harbored about whether heaven and hell are real.

These arguments—for proof of the reality of heaven and hell—require an understanding of the gospel message. Here is how we explain it in 151 words: *God created humanity for the purpose of having an intimate, eternal relationship with them. But because of humanity's sin, that relationship was severed. There was only one way for the relationship to be restored: God's Son, the perfect and holy Jesus, had to die to pay the penalty for each human's sin. Jesus died on the cross in our place so that we could be saved from the judgment and penalty of eternal suffering for our rejection and rebellion against God. That offer of salvation is available to any and all who, during their lifetime, repent of their sins and make Christ the central focus of their life (which is an appropriate response to the love shown by Christ to die for us). Those who accept the offer of Christ's salvation will spend their physical lifetime in fellowship with the almighty God, and the eternity of their afterlife in his presence.*

Jesus also explained the gospel message, but he did it more succinctly than we did (after all, he is Jesus). Here, in 117 words, is how Jesus explained the gospel to a Jewish religious leader (Nicodemus):

> "This is how much God loved the world: He gave his Son, his one and only Son. And this is why: so that no one need be destroyed; by believing in him, anyone can have a whole and lasting life. God didn't go to all the trouble of sending his Son merely to point an accusing finger, telling the world how bad it was. He came to help, to put the world right again. Anyone who trusts in him is acquitted; anyone who refuses to trust him has long since been under the death sentence without knowing it. And why? Because of that person's failure to believe in the one-of-a-kind Son of God when introduced to him."

John 3:16–18 THE MESSAGE

With that understanding, let's move to the two arguments:

Heaven must exist—because Jesus went to the cross

Jesus is looking forward to being with us in heaven. He endured the suffering and death of the cross so that our eternity could be with him, or, as he phrased it to his disciples, "that where I am you may be also" (John 14:3 ESV).

If that wasn't true—if there is no heaven, no arrangement for us to be in God's presence for eternity—then Jesus didn't have to die. He could have *skipped* the whole brutality, suffering, torture, and crucifixion. If there was no heaven, then there was no need for the cross.

But he *did* endure it. Why? Logic and reason dictate that he died for us because heaven is real. And the cross was the only way to get us there.

Hell must exist—because Jesus went to the cross

Similarly, or is it conversely, hell must exist. If not, why would Jesus choose to die? If there was no risk that any of us would suffer judgment and an agonizing eternal separation from God—if there was no eternal penalty for our sin—Jesus could have avoided the cross altogether. No need to go through that excruciating experience on our behalf if we were not facing any disastrous consequences.

But he *did* endure the pain of the cross. Why? Logic and reason dictate that he died for us because hell is real. The cross was the only way to get us out of there.

QUESTIONS FOR REFLECTION AND DISCUSSION

- Can you summarize the gospel message in fewer than 117 words?
- What is your response or retort to these two arguments?

4

Can I Believe What the Bible Says About the End of the World?

Introduction

In 2009, Los Angeles residents were startled by numerous billboards declaring,

2012: We Were Warned

As it turned out, that was just prerelease hype for the end-of-the-world disaster film *2012*, which had great special effects but a plot that couldn't sustain the 158-minute runtime. On the positive side, the film educated us about the Maya calendar. (That isn't cinematic fiction; there really is one.) According to the movie's plot, the ancient calendar of pre-Columbian Mesoamerica predicted the end of the world on December 21, 2012, and the movie portrayed all of the requisite events for that apocalyptic date (volcanic eruptions, earthquakes, and tsunamis, which befell John Cusack and his kids).

Thirty-five months after the movie's release, on the actual day of December 21, 2012, nothing happened. But by then there was enough curiosity about the Maya calendar that the National Aeronautics and Space Administration issued a news release on December 22, 2012, stating that (1) the world didn't end on December 21, and (2) there were no Maya calendar predictions for the end of the world on that date.[1] NASA explained that December 21, 2012, was a significant day in Maya theology, but it was not a date of destruction. Bottom line: People were simply misreading the Maya calendar, finding a prediction of global destruction where none was implied.

Interestingly, another set of billboards appeared across the nation during 2009 and 2010, proclaiming that God's judgment day was coming on May 21, 2011, and that the "Bible guaranteed it." Organized by evangelist Harold Camping, his well-advertised judgment day had to be recalibrated to October 21 when May 21 turned out to be uneventful. You probably don't remember October 21, 2011, because it was also unmemorable. After those successive humiliations, Harold Camping issued a public apology, asking forgiveness for his "sinful" predictions. His letter began:

> Events within the last year have proven that no man can be fully trusted. Even the most sincere and zealous of us can be mistaken.[2]

Yes, Camping was untrustworthy, but what about God? Can we believe what the Bible says about the end of the world? Or is it as easily misunderstood as the Maya calendar?

■ ▓ ▪

Most people have a curiosity about *if* or *how* the world is going to end. Many people are fascinated by the subject. If you are intrigued by it, congratulations. The Bible tells us this is a worthwhile subject for us to contemplate:

> You learn more at a funeral than at a feast—after all, that's where we'll end up. We might discover something from it.
>
> Ecclesiastes 7:2 THE MESSAGE

This verse speaks to the subject of dying: The time to think about death is while you are still alive, because after you are dead, it will be too late. And the same principle applies to the subject of the end of the world (often referred to as the end times). Think about the end times now, because—according to the Bible—your eternal destiny is determined by the decisions you make during your lifetime. But your conclusions and decisions regarding the end times will only be as good as the trustworthiness of the information on which you are relying. So it is entirely appropriate to ask if you can believe what the Bible says about the end times.

Before we examine the Bible's commentary on the end times, we need to talk about the distinction between predictions and biblical prophecies:

Predictions: Any person can make one. It can be about the weather, the outcome of a sporting event, or the opening price of an IPO stock. And let's not forget about predictions of eschatological (end-times) events. As discussed above, Harold Camping was big on making predictions about the rapture and judgment day. But he was terrible at it; never got one right. That's the thing about predictions—they come with no guarantee of accuracy. Predictions are a crapshoot.

Prophecy: As used in the Bible, a prophecy carries the weight of God's word. God spoke through his designated representatives. In the Old Testament, prophets primarily engaged in *forthtelling*: speaking God's word to God's people about God's own nature or about their spiritual condition. But the Old Testament prophets are perhaps more famous for what they did less often: *foretelling* the details of a future event. This wasn't an ability that they displayed at social gatherings for people's amusement. Their prophecies always related to events within God's plans and were only issued as God granted ability to the prophets, and they always proved true. For example:

- Micah correctly foretold that the temple of Solomon in Jerusalem would be destroyed (Micah 3:12).

- Jeremiah accurately prophesied that the Babylonian captivity would last only seventy years (Jeremiah 25:11; 29:10).

In the first century AD, there were no official prophets, but God used other spokesmen who prophesied about the end times. Jesus taught frequently about hell and described the signs that will precede the end times; what he said qualifies as the words of God because he was the Son of God. The apostles Paul, Peter, and John each wrote portions of the New Testament, and they received the inspiration of the Holy Spirit of God to do so (2 Timothy 3:16).

- The apostles Paul and Peter explained the rapture to those first-century Christians and encouraged them to be faithful while waiting for Christ's second coming.
- The apostle John, while exiled and imprisoned by the Roman government on the island of Patmos, wrote the book of Revelation (the last book in the Bible); written in about AD 95, the book is a transcription of the visions that John received from God about the events that will happen at the end of the world.

The sayings of Jesus and writings of John, Peter, and Paul about future events of the end times carry the same weight as prophecy. What you read in the New Testament, like what is written in the Old Testament, came directly from God. As Dr. R. C. Sproul explains it:

> The Holy Spirit guided the human authors so that their words would be nothing less than the word of God. How God superintended the original writings of the Bible is not known. But inspiration does not mean that God dictated his messages to those who wrote the Bible. Rather, the Holy Spirit communicated through the human writers the very words of God.[3]

In the Bible's chronology, any biblical promise of something that is yet to occur in the future rises to the level of God-spoken,

God-guaranteed prophecy. As the Bible presents them, these are not merely predictions. Rather, they are certainties that have not yet occurred.

QUESTIONS FOR REFLECTION AND DISCUSSION

- Do you agree that considering life-after-death and related end-times issues is a worthwhile endeavor?
- What would you hope to gain from such a study?
- Should prophecies in the Bible be given equal, less, or more weight than predictions from any other source?

Testing the Bible's Veracity

How can we verify prophecies about end-times events that have not yet occurred?

If the world never ends during your lifetime, you won't get a chance to verify the biblical prophecies. However, if the world actually comes to an end—and if you are still alive to witness it—then you'll probably be too busy dodging cataclysmic disasters (like John Cusack in the *2012* movie) to pull out your pocket guide to biblical end-times prophecies. While we can't test the veracity of biblical prophecies that haven't occurred, we can check the Bible's track record for prophecies that have a completed lifespan.

What is the Bible's track record with other prophecies in general?

World-renowned astrophysicist Dr. Hugh Ross has already applied his considerable mathematical and scientific brainpower to this specific assignment.[4] Dr. Ross determined that the Bible contains approximately 2,500 prophecies. He has confirmed that approximately 2,000 have been fulfilled to the letter, exactly as prophesied, in most cases centuries after the prophecy was made. (There remain about 500 that involve events which have not yet occurred, those being the end-times prophecies). According to Dr. Ross, the probability of any one of the prophecies coming true is less than 1 in 10. The chances that all 2,000 prophecies could have happened just by chance, for the most part independent of each other, without any error, is less than 1 in 10 to the 2,000th power. Since any probability greater than 1 in 10 to the 50th power is considered impossible, there is only one reasonable explanation for the complete accuracy of the Bible prophecies: God made the prophecies, and God fulfilled them.

What's the Bible's track record with the specific messianic prophecies?

Our minds are boggled when the exponent is to the 2,000th power. So let's narrow our focus to the already-occurred prophecies regarding a single theme: the Messiah. Throughout the Old Testament, God promised the Jews that He would send a king to establish God's kingdom on earth. This "deliverer" was referred to as the Messiah. Bible researchers have identified 365 specific messianic prophecies, made by different authors of the Old Testament, spanning thousands of years, all written long before the birth of Christ, yet all of which have been fulfilled by Jesus Christ as reported in the New Testament.[5]

The Jews were confident that the Messiah would come, but they didn't want to miss him. So the messianic prophecies were important and precious to the Jews because they provided some fairly specific clues about the identity of the Messiah. Here is a portion of the checklist the Jews were working from (for each, we've listed the verse in which the prophecy was made and the verse revealing that Jesus fulfilled the prophecy):

- *City of birth*—He was going to be born in the hick town of Bethlehem (Micah 5:2; Luke 2:4, 6–7).

- *Distinguishing characteristics*—As strange as it seems, the Messiah would be born to a virgin (Isaiah 7:4; Matthew 1:18, 22–23).

- *Childhood*—Although born in Bethlehem, he would spend His childhood in Egypt (Hosea 11:1 and Isaiah 9:6; Matthew 2:13–23).

- *Notoriety*—He would have a ceremonial entrance into Jerusalem on a donkey (Zechariah 9:9; Matthew 21:2, 4–5).

- *Death*—He would die by crucifixion, the method reserved for the most heinous criminals (Psalm 34:20; John 19:16–30).

- *Famous last words*—Even the Messiah's dying words were predicted (Psalm 22:1; Mark 15:34).

- *Resurrection from the dead*—As if the virgin birth wasn't enough, the Messiah would come back to life after his death (Psalm 16:9–10; Acts 2:31).

Mathematician and college professor Peter W. Stoner ran some calculations to determine the odds of each of eight of the messianic prophecies being fulfilled, and then he extrapolated the odds of the *same person* matching all eight. His findings determined that "the chance that any man might have lived down to the present time and fulfilled all eight prophecies is 1 in 10 to the 17th power."[6] Those odds are 1 in 100 quadrillion. Written out, that number is 100,000,000,000,000,000. We appreciate that Stoner provided a visual illustration as a means of explaining the odds of this immensity to us nonmathematicians:

Suppose that we take 10^{17} silver dollars and lay them on the face of Texas. They will cover all of the state two feet deep. Now mark one of these silver dollars and stir the whole mass thoroughly, all over the state. Blindfold a man and tell him that he can travel as far as he wishes, but he must pick up one silver dollar and say that this is the right one. What chance would he have of getting the right one? Just the same chance that the prophets would have had of writing these eight prophecies and having them all come true in any one man, from their day to the present time, providing they wrote using their own wisdom.[7]

What *Does* the Bible Say About the End of the World?

While we can't verify the Bible's end-times prophecies before they happen, it might be helpful for you to know what they are (so you can recognize them if they start to happen). Here is an oversimplified, condensed version of biblical end-times highlights:

Rapture: At an unknown time, Jesus Christ will appear in the sky and all Christians, living and dead, will be transported to meet him. It will happen in a blink of an eye.

Tribulation: A three-and-a-half-year period of peace and harmony on earth (except for the natural disasters) is an illusion perpetrated by the Antichrist (who is in cahoots with Satan). In the second three and a half years, the Antichrist unleashes a campaign of horrors.

Armageddon: As the Tribulation ends, this will be the world's last and worst war. A coalition of nations under the Antichrist will prepare for battle against a two-hundred-million-soldier army from the east.

The second coming: As the great battle of Armageddon is about to begin, Jesus Christ will return to earth to take his place as the rightful King. His armies from heaven prevail over the Antichrist and the armies of the earth.

The millennium: The millennium kingdom is a period of one thousand years when there will be peace on earth. As with most end-times events, there is disagreement over the reality and/or timing of the millennium kingdom.

The judgment seat of Christ: This judgment is reserved for people who were committed followers of Jesus. No guilt or innocence determinations here. It is a reward ceremony for faithful service.

Great white throne judgment: This is the scary one if you are not a follower of Christ. All people from throughout history will be brought to this judgment for their rejection of God.

Don't expect to find a list like this in the Bible. End-times prophecies are scattered throughout the Old and New Testaments. They are not arranged in a singular, chronological presentation. Many of the descriptions (particularly in the book of Revelation) are most likely literal, but others appear to be metaphorical. It is difficult to determine which is which. Remember that John's vision could have been of something commonplace today (such as a military fighter jet), which would have been incomprehensible to his first-century mind. The result: a vision of something literal that was described by words that seem metaphorical.

Let's face it. God could have made all of this more easily understood. But he chose not to. God is keeping much of this a mystery, keeping our vision of the future veiled. The apostle Paul explained our restricted knowledge of future events with this verse:

> For now we see only a reflection as in a mirror; then we shall see face to face. Now I know in part; then I shall know fully, even as I am fully known.
>
> 1 Corinthians 13:12

Likewise, God is intentionally keeping his timetable for all of this a secret. Scripture is silent about when the end times kick in.

If some religious goofball predicts a certain date for the rapture, you can be sure it won't happen on that day. As Jesus himself said:

> "But about that day or hour no one knows, not even the angels in heaven, nor the Son, but only the Father."
>
> Matthew 24:36

Clues! Can't We at Least Have a Few Clues?

God gives us only a fuzzy view of the future, and he won't tell us when it is going to happen. But couldn't he at least give us a few clues or signs to determine if the end times are approaching? The good news is that he has. The bad news is that he gave these signs to his disciples about two thousand years ago. But maybe these clues seem a little more relevant to us today than they were two thousand years ago. In Matthew 24, the disciples approach Jesus and blurt out the same question that haunts us: "What sign will signal your return and the end of the world?" (Mathew 24:3 NLT).

In response, Jesus gives a list of global events and circumstances that will be "only the first of the birth pains, with more to come" (Matthew 24:8 NLT). Here's a partial list of the signs he said would precede the end times. You'll need to ask yourself if these clues are apparent today (and we can't resist giving you a hint):

- An increase in earthquakes. (Hint: Pacific Rim.)
- Wars and rumors of more wars. (Hint: Are you watching any news channel?)
- Famines. (Hint: Think of East Africa, Yemen, and South Sudan.)
- The persecution of Christians. (Hint: The mass slaughters of Syrian Christians.)
- An increase in wickedness. (Think ISIS beheadings and the Boko Haram kidnapping of 276 schoolgirls.)

- The gospel of Jesus Christ will be preached around the world. (Hint: Satellite TV and the Internet).

If you want signs, these are the things Jesus said to look for. Perhaps you'll agree with the apostle Paul, who stated that Christ's return is imminent (it could happen at any time), although it might not be immediate.

But because we don't know when these things will commence, we shouldn't be lulled into a sense of complacency about them. It could happen when we least expect it. As Paul explained:

> For you know very well that the day of the Lord will come like a thief in the night. While people are saying, "Peace and safety," destruction will come on them suddenly, as labor pains on a pregnant woman, and they will not escape.
>
> 1 Thessalonians 5:2–3

Awareness of God's plan for the end of the world is important, but it is not essential. As far as your eternity is concerned—the timing of the Tribulation, whether the millennium is literal or symbolic, whether Christians go through the Tribulation—none of these questions matter. If these things were essential to your salvation, God would have explained them in more detail. But he didn't. Instead of being obsessed with the end times, God wants us obsessed with Jesus and his love for us. He wants us to realize that our salvation is not predicated on escaping the Tribulation but upon God's grace and our faith in Jesus Christ. Nothing more, nothing less.

> For it is by grace you have been saved, through faith—and this is not from yourselves, it is the gift of God—not by works, so that no one can boast. For we are God's handiwork, created in Christ Jesus to do good works, which God prepared in advance for us to do.
>
> Ephesians 2:8–10

QUESTIONS FOR REFLECTION AND DISCUSSION

- Do you feel better knowing what Jesus identified as signs of the impending end times?
- Will you live differently in any manner knowing this information?
- Do you consider the Matthew 24 list of early warning signs to be trustworthy?

5

Do All Roads Lead to Heaven?

Introduction

Ari is a relatively new Christian. He was raised by a mother who attends church regularly and a father who, though not antagonistic to faith, is not a participant in it. Over the last two years Ari has sought to find more meaning in life and has connected with his local church. He's grown to trust that Jesus is God, and that the greatest goal for his life is to love God and love his neighbors. Through many ups and downs, Ari has grown in prayer and obedience to Christ.

Recently, Ari's willingness to wrestle with the important questions of faith and life led to a conversation about the road to heaven. Over coffee he asked this poignant question: "What happens to the Hindu boy raised in rural India who is taught by his parents to seek something higher but has never heard the name of Jesus? Does he go to heaven? After all, he's religious and believes in the only transcendent thing he's ever known."

Ari's excellent question raises several others:

- What about the girl whose father is a Muslim and taught her to worship Allah and respect Jesus as simply a prophet?
- What about the Jewish kid in Israel who is taught the Torah, believes in God, but has learned to reject Jesus as the Messiah?
- Or for that matter, what about the young people in the good ol' U.S.A. who never step foot in a church, are raised by unbelieving parents, are educated in secular schools, but are taught to be good, obey the law, and respect people?

Ari is wrestling with a question many of us ask. Do all religious roads lead to heaven? Do the devout have a place in paradise? Don't all good people (and dogs) go to heaven?

Ari said it this way: "I believe Jesus is God and is our Savior. But my mom introduced me to the idea very early. Church was always on my radar. And now I've found him for myself. But it doesn't seem right that someone else, traveling a different road to God, is missing out simply because they have a different map."

■ ▓ ■

Of all the questions we're dealing with in this book about heaven and hell, this one is most commonly asked by both Christians and non-Christians: Do all roads lead to heaven? By "roads" we mean "religions," but even that may not be a broad enough category to cover everyone who's ever given serious thought to their life and what happens when they die. Even people with no religious affiliation ask this question.

In chapter 2 we gave you the Christian answer to the question "What happens when you die?" But our response may not be enough to satisfy every perspective. It certainly isn't broad enough for those who question the Bible's truth and authority. If you believe the Bible is just another book written by imperfect people, then of course you would have reason to doubt its teaching on the subject of the afterlife.

Or maybe you're like our friend Ari, who has recently come to believe in Jesus and wants to follow him, but wonders why God would exclude those who are sincerely seeking him just because they are using a different map.

In past generations, becoming a Christian was like joining an exclusive club. Only those who believed in and followed the club rules could be members, and only the members (those who were "saved") were going to heaven. Unfortunately, this way of believing often led to a smugness on the part of the members. They felt privileged even if they didn't keep all the rules. In fact, rule keeping was secondary. What mattered most was that they were members, and they were going to heaven no matter what. The rest of the world—all those who weren't in the club—had to fend for themselves. Once in a while the club members felt sorry for those who were members of the "wrong" religions and therefore would be denied access to heaven. But mostly they felt good about themselves because they were definitely going to heaven.

Thankfully, such a distorted view of what it means to be a Christian—Tim Keller accurately calls it "deadly triumphalism"[1]—has fallen out of favor with Christians today. Like Ari, many of those who follow Christ don't feel any exclusivity. If anything, they take comfort in knowing they are going to heaven, but they wonder about those around them who believe they are going to heaven, even though they are on a different road.

Love Wins?

In his book *Love Wins*, Rob Bell expressed his own struggle with the exclusive claims of Christianity. In fact, he was motivated to write the book when he overheard someone state that Mahatma Gandhi, the famous Hindu peace activist, wasn't going to heaven. Bell found that conclusion preposterous, prompting him to conduct a theological and moral investigation of the doctrine of heaven and hell. His conclusion that everybody was going to heaven in the end ignited a firestorm of controversy.

Bell's view, known as universalism, isn't new. Various theologians and Christian thinkers through the centuries have promoted the idea that everyone will gain access to heaven in one form or another. Until *Love Wins* became a bestselling book, however, the view wasn't taken all that seriously by modern readers. But Rob Bell's skill as a communicator and writer, coupled with the growing desire of Christians—especially young adults—to make God more palatable and less vindictive, has given rise to the current angst over heaven's perceived exclusivity.

We use the word *angst* deliberately, because the idea that those who haven't accepted God's one-way plan of salvation would go to hell creates anxiety in a lot of people, Christians included. They count it a privilege to be among those who are going to heaven, but they dislike the concept of exclusivity. Like Ari, they don't think it's right that someone else, traveling on a different road to God, is missing out simply because they have a different "map."

QUESTIONS FOR REFLECTION AND DISCUSSION

- Do you identify with Ari's concern about the exclusivity of Christianity? Why or why not?
- Expand on Tim Keller's phrase "deadly triumphalism." What does that mean, and how has this attitude hurt the Christian cause?
- Why would God have only one way to reach him?

The Difference between Maps and Roads

Maps are wonderful things, but they don't always tell the whole story. With the proliferation of smartphones and map apps, you can easily chart a route from the place you are to the place you want to go. All you need is the address of the final destination. The map app will usually suggest the quickest route, but it's often not the only route. There are other ways you could follow to get to your destination. You just have to choose another route. It may not be as direct, but you eventually get to where you want to go.

There's only one problem with maps. They are useful, but ultimately a map is nothing more than a guide. You can't travel on a map. For that you need a road. So lets talk about roads

The reason there appear to be so many roads to heaven is that there are so many different religions, each one claiming to have an exclusive way to know God and therefore an exclusive way to heaven, where God lives. If each religion or belief is a road, and they all claim to offer the best way to heaven, how do you sort them all out? Why should you even care? What business is it of yours that others believe differently? Why not live and let live?

That's fine if all religions are essentially the same. But what if they aren't? In fact, a cursory study of the world's major religions will tell you that they are not the same. To the contrary, religions by their very nature are mutually exclusive. Each religion believes it is the only one that's true, which is impossible since each religion offers a different road to heaven. Therefore, it would be more intellectually honest to say all religions are *wrong* than to say they are all right. Which brings us back to the prospect that there is only one true religion and just one road or one way to believe in God that leads to heaven.

If this is true, it has profound implications. If there's just one true road to God, the roads offered by other religions and belief systems are false. But it's worse than that. If there's just one road that leads to life, then the other roads—no matter how right they seem—lead to death. All of them.

We know, this is harsh. But it's what the Bible says in pretty much the same way: "There is a way that appears to be right, but in the end it leads to death" (Proverbs 14:12).

What Is the Only Way?

All of this is fine in theory, you might be saying, but how do you discover the only true way, the one that leads to life? The Christian

69

answer to this question is actually quite simple: Jesus is the one true way. In fact, he said so very clearly:

> "I am the way and the truth and the life. No one comes to the Father except through me."

John 14:6

The reason Christians can say "This is the only way to God and heaven" is that Jesus said it first. In fact, before the followers of Jesus were called Christians (Acts 11:26), they were called men and women of "the Way" (Acts 9:2). And they were persecuted for it.

You see, Jesus came into a world where there were many "ways" to God and eternal life. Early Christians were called atheists by the occupying Roman government because they worshiped only one God rather than the many gods of Roman mythology, not to mention the god the Romans hailed as Caesar. Those who followed Jesus Christ exclusively were going against the grain of culture. And they paid a price for their beliefs in an exclusive Way.

Things aren't all that different today. We may not be experiencing persecution in the West, but Christians in many parts of the world are being persecuted and killed for believing in Jesus as the only way. And in our own free society, those who share that belief and claim to have exclusive truth are often accused of being intolerant and bigoted.

The Exclusivity of Jesus

The philosopher Peter Kreeft gives us a clue as to why cultures both ancient and modern have rejected this exclusivity and the people who embraced it. "If 'One Way' is bigotry, then it is Jesus who is the bigot. He smacks us full in the face with the stark either-or acceptance or rejection. No side roads."[2]

It isn't just the claim Jesus made to being the only road to heaven that has offended people. In his book *Everything You Ever Wanted to Know About Heaven,* Kreeft lists the five teachings of Jesus that most scandalize the human mind, both ancient and modern:

1. Sin
2. Hell
3. His claim to divinity
4. Miracles
5. His "One Way" exclusivity[3]

Against these teachings, people have always preferred to believe in

1. The natural goodness of the human race
2. Universal salvation
3. A merely human Christ
4. Natural rather than supernatural occurrences
5. The equality of all religions[4]

Why is that? Why don't people want to accept what Jesus really taught? Why do they struggle with Jesus as he really is? Kreeft says it's the claims to exclusivity that bother people most about Christ and Christianity. Yet we don't apply that thinking to things like politics, scientific theories, or media reports. We test them to find out what is really true and what is not. We don't accept that all political candidates are the same, or that different scientific theories are all correct, or that differing media reports about the same incident are all true. We want to know which candidate is speaking the truth, which scientific theory is correct, and which story is accurate.

So why do we insist that two or more religions, each of which presents a different road or way to God, are equally valid? There's only one explanation. We don't think religion is about truth. "We embrace the equality of religions only because we embrace the equality of myths," writes Kreeft.[5] *The Lord of the Rings* is no more or less true than *Star Wars* or the Bible because they are all made up.

But if the Bible is a myth, then Jesus is a myth, and everything he said is a lie. Of course, even the critics of Christianity don't go that far. They're okay with Jesus as a great moral teacher, as long as you take out the supernatural elements, such as his miracles, his exclusive claim to be God, and the resurrection. But that doesn't work either, as C. S. Lewis famously argued in *Mere Christianity*:

> I am trying here to prevent anyone saying the really foolish thing that people often say about Him: "I'm ready to accept Jesus as a great moral teacher, but I don't accept His claim to be God." That is the one thing we must not say. A man who was merely a man and said the sort of things Jesus said would not be a great moral teacher. He would either be a lunatic—on a level with the man who says he is a poached egg—or else he would be the Devil of Hell. You must make your choice. Either this man was, and is, the Son of God: or else a madman or something worse. You can shut Him up for a fool, you can spit at Him and kill Him as a demon; or you can fall at His feet and call Him Lord and God. But let us not come with any patronizing nonsense about His being a great human teacher. He has not left that open to us. He did not intend to.[6]

No less an authority than the apostle Paul was even more direct: "If Christ has not been raised, your faith is futile" (1 Corinthians 15:17). In other words, why would you even bother to follow someone who's dead? "If only for this life we have hope in Christ," Paul continued, "we are of all people most to be pitied" (verse 19).

QUESTIONS FOR REFLECTION AND DISCUSSION

- Reflect on the five teachings of Jesus that most "scandalize" the human mind. Explain why you agree or disagree with the five alternate views embraced by contemporary cultures.
- Why do people struggle with Jesus' claiming to be exclusive, and yet we readily accept claims of exclusivity in other fields, such as science and journalism?

- From your understanding of the world's three great monotheistic religions—Christianity, Judaism, and Islam—what is one "mutually exclusive" belief in each one?

No Man-Made Road Reaches Heaven

The resurrection of Jesus is not just a compelling reason to accept his claim to be the only way to God; it's an essential reason. And yet you may still be uncomfortable with the claim of exclusivity. You don't want to sound bigoted or imperialistic. And yes, it would be "sheer imperialism to insist that only one man-made road up the divine mountain is the right road and all the others are wrong."[7]

But the story of Jesus isn't like the other stories in the other religions. The Way of Jesus is completely unique. In every other story of every other religion—with no exception—the way you get to heaven is by your good works. The five pillars of Islam, the mandatory service of Mormon missionaries, the good deeds of Hinduism—all of them talk about people taking a road to heaven paved with works.

Christianity alone says that our works contribute nothing to our acceptance by God. Therefore, there is nothing we can do to reach God from our level. No matter how many roads we build heavenward, none of them will reach God. Every other religion claims to be a road to God. That's not what Christianity is. Christianity is the road God made to us. "That's why the 'One Way' claim is necessary," writes Kreeft, "because we are only repeating the message God gave us—we are mailmen, not authors."[8] The message is clear: There is no way up from us to God, but there is one way down.

Think of yourself as drowning in the open sea. You aren't wearing a life vest. The water is rough and you are out of options. Just as you are going down for the last time, a rescue helicopter appears above you and lets down a ladder. It's your only option, your only way to live. You grab the ladder that's been lowered for you and climb to safety.

Maybe we're being a little obvious, but we have to say it: Jesus is the ladder that's been lowered by God in order to rescue us and take us to safety, to heaven. That's not just us talking. Jesus said it of himself: "Very truly I tell you, you will see 'heaven open, and the angels of God ascending and descending on the Son of Man'" (John 1:51).

We could end this chapter here and be satisfied that we have adequately answered the question "Do all roads lead to heaven?" But we're not quite finished because we have a feeling you don't find the answer completely satisfying. You may believe in your head that Jesus is the only way to God, but in your heart you may still feel uncomfortable with the exclusivity of your belief. We get it. No one—least of all Christians—wants to appear arrogant. We have far too much of that in the history of Christianity. We want to show more love and less judgment. In that spirit, we want to consider three additional questions:

- Is there more than one way to Jesus?
- Does believing in Jesus marginalize others?
- Is God's plan fair?

Is There More Than One Way to Jesus?

Jesus insists and Christians believe that he is the only way to God, but is it possible that there are many ways to Jesus? Peter Kreeft asks the question this way: "What subjective relationship must one have with Jesus in order to be on the right way?"[9] Some insist you merely need to say a prayer inviting Jesus into your heart. Others suggest it isn't enough to reduce your salvation to a "magic formula," that there needs to be true repentance, or a desire to turn away from sin. But was the thief on the cross next to Jesus sorry for his sins? All we know from the text is that he said, "Jesus, remember me when you come into your kingdom," to which Jesus answered, "Truly I tell you, today you will be with me in paradise" (Luke 23:42–43).

What about the Old Testament saints? How were they saved? James the apostle, writing about the kind of faith it takes to please God, said that "Abraham believed God, and it was credited to him as righteousness" (James 2:23). Abraham didn't know Jesus, but he experienced the righteousness of God extended to sinful people through Jesus.

John the apostle opens his Gospel with a grand description of Jesus as the preincarnate Word, "the true light that gives light to everyone" (John 1:9) who "became flesh and made his dwelling among us" (verse 14). According to John, how do you "receive" the true light and become a child of God? By believing in his name (John 1:12).

What about your mind? How much knowledge about God and Jesus do you need to have in order to be saved? The apostle Paul walked around the city of Athens and noticed an object of worship with the inscription "To an unknown God" (Acts 17:23). He called the Athenians ignorant and proceeded to give them a description of the one true creator God (verses 24–28). In the past, Paul said, "God overlooked such ignorance, but now he commands all people everywhere to repent. For he has set a day when he will judge the world with justice by the man he has appointed. He has given proof of this to everyone by raising him from the dead" (verses 30–31).

And don't get us started on the miraculous ways people are being saved in different parts of the world today. There are many well-documented examples of Muslim people encountering the living Christ through dreams. In his bestselling book *Seeking Allah, Finding Jesus*, Nabeel Qureshi tells his amazing story of having all the knowledge about God he could possibly want. But it wasn't until he had a series of three dreams that he was convinced to put his faith in Jesus as his Savior and Lord.

So how do non-Christians come to know Christ unto salvation? Do they "receive" Jesus into their hearts? Do they believe in his name? Does it happen when there's enough knowledge to understand that it is the resurrection of Christ that ensures our salvation? The answer to all of these questions is a resounding yes. Salvation by faith in Jesus is not as straightforward or formulaic as we think.

Maybe you did nothing more than pray a simple prayer that *asked Jesus into your heart.* Or perhaps you wrestled for years, not sure of what it takes to *surrender your life to Christ.* Or maybe you grew into your faith and can't pinpoint a moment when you *accepted Jesus as your Lord and Savior.* The bottom line is that you know because your life has changed. You aren't the same person you were before. Something supernatural has happened to you that can only be explained by the presence of Jesus in your life.

QUESTIONS FOR REFLECTION AND DISCUSSION

- Explain how the Way of Jesus is completely unique among the world's religions and belief systems.
- Expand on Peter Kreeft's statement "We are mailmen, not authors."
- Describe your relationship with Jesus Christ. What words would you use to explain how you came to have a relationship in the first place?

Does Believing in Jesus Marginalize Others?

In his book *The Case for the Real Jesus,* Lee Strobel asks two questions that go to the heart of our discussion on the exclusivity of Jesus and Christianity. "When one religion, like Christianity, claims a unique path to salvation," he writes, "doesn't that inevitably lead to marginalizing and persecuting people who believe otherwise?" Furthermore, "Is common ground for discussion even possible when one group claims a monopoly on truth?"[10]

One of the main criticisms leveled against Christians is that they are intolerant of other viewpoints. Christians are more sensitive of this label of intolerance than they were in the past. We certainly are. But does that mean we have to compromise our beliefs in order to gain a hearing with those who disagree with us?

Strobel interviewed Paul Copan, a professor of philosophy who has written more than a dozen books on Christian belief. Responding to the two questions on marginalization, Copan offers some helpful advice:[11]

- All truth is God's truth, so Christians don't have a truth monopoly. It's possible to agree with someone on important moral and social issues, even if we don't agree theologically.

- If there ever was a person who did not marginalize people, it was Jesus. He reached out to those who were marginalized and was accused by his opponents of being a friend to sinners (imagine that). The truth is that God doesn't want anyone to die in their sins, but wants everyone to "come to repentance" (2 Peter 3:9). Just because that doesn't happen doesn't mean God is marginalizing them. If anything, those who refuse his plan to save sinners through Jesus are marginalizing God.

- It's not truth that marginalizes people; it's people who marginalize people. You can have a productive conversation and respect someone who disagrees with you. Dr. Barry Corey, president of Biola University, urges Christians to have "firm centers and soft edges."[12] You can keep a core of conviction without marginalizing those you disagree with. This is what the apostle Paul has in mind when he advises Christians, "If it is possible, as far as it depends on you, live at peace with everyone" (Romans 12:18).

Is God's Plan Fair?

In his excellent book *The Heaven Promise*, Scot McKnight encourages us to keep two things in mind about God and his "exclusive" plan. One, God is perfectly and eternally good, so what he does is fair, even if it doesn't seem that way to us. Two, this perfectly good God loves all human beings equally. McKnight writes,

> We don't know how God makes these opportunities possible for each person in history—past, present, and future. But we can trust the God of promise to accomplish what he wants to do because this God is good and this God is loving.[13]

One of the distinctives of Christianity is that it offers just one way to God, but that one way is available to every single person. Nobody is exempt and no one is excluded.

Why Are People Reluctant to Follow Jesus?

It would be great if everyone viewed God in the same way, as a good and loving Father in heaven who has our best interest in mind at all times, who doesn't want anyone to perish. We'd even be happy if the majority of people believed in God that way. But that just isn't the case. If anything, there is a reluctance in the vast majority of people to believe God and follow Jesus. Have you ever thought about this? Why don't more people believe?

The philosopher Douglas Geivett provides an answer we find satisfying, even though it's simple. All the evidence about God, both from history and from experience, suggests a God who understands the human condition. "However, God's interest in us and his initiative toward us respects our capacity for self-determination as free creatures," Geivett writes. "Thus, we find members of the human community resisting God's attempts to establish lines of communication with himself."[14] Certainly God could have created us without free will, so that we had no choice but to accept him. But that would be inconsistent with his loving nature. God loves us too much to force us into a decision. But that leaves the door open for people to refuse him. A lot of people.

If you have not resisted God's attempts to communicate with you, and you have accepted the truth of his plan to freely offer salvation through Jesus—including his life, death, and resurrection—but you still find the exclusive nature of that plan to be unsettling, here's an elegant suggestion from Geivett. "If you think the Christian worldview is reasonable, but your heart has not caught up with your mind, you need to understand that it's a normal part of spiritual development in the Christian way."[15]

What Geivett is suggesting is that a reluctance to follow Christ fully is usually emotional rather than intellectual. He's not saying, and neither are we, that you should disregard rational thought. But neither should you rely completely on reason. Christianity is a reasonable faith, but we come to faith by trusting with our hearts as much as we do believing with our minds. As Philip Yancey so eloquently states, "Faith means believing in advance what will only make sense in reverse."[16]

Why faith? The writer of Hebrews puts it this way: "Without faith it is impossible to please God, because anyone who comes to him must believe that he exists and that he rewards those who earnestly seek him" (Hebrews 11:6).

Take the next step in faith and see what God will do.

QUESTIONS FOR REFLECTION AND DISCUSSION

- Give an example of a time when you were tempted to compromise your beliefs in order to gain a hearing with someone who disagreed with you.
- Give an example of a time when you stayed firm in your convictions but were able to relate to someone you disagreed with.
- Why are people reluctant to follow Jesus? Why don't more people believe?
- Explain how God's giving us the ability to accept or reject him comes out of his love for us.

6

If God Is Loving, How Could He Send Anyone to Hell?

Introduction

The college group at St. Andrew's Presbyterian Church is a small but feisty group of believers who meet weekly to build relationships and discover more of God together. A couple of years ago they went through an eight-week gathering simply titled "Questions." Each week they selected a biblical topic, the students anonymously scribbled their questions on the topic that were most troubling to them, and then the leaders of the college ministry read the questions and began the discussion.

An interesting thing happened on the night that hell was the topic. Most of the submissions asked the same question (which were worded almost identically): "If God is loving, how can he send anyone to hell?"

This question plagues most millennials who are curious about the Christian faith, but it is not limited to that age demographic.

The same question haunts people on the other end of the age spectrum, as evidenced by this letter we recently received:

> Dear Bruce and Stan:
>
> I'm close to eighty years old. I became a Christian as a kid and never thought much about hell. It was in the Bible. Jesus taught about it. So I believed it.
>
> It's only in the last few years that I've been troubled by the doctrine of hell. Why would God create a system wherein some (probably a lot of) people will be tortured for eternity in a place called hell? That doesn't sound like a very loving thing to do, does it?[1]

Great question, right? And as these two examples illustrate, it is as perplexing to Christians as it is to atheists, agnostics, and other nonbelievers who are simply trying to figure out Christianity.

■ ▓ ■

As young kids, we were raised in an era when biblical doctrine was revered by churchgoers, and even the nonchurch world included evidence of Judeo-Christian influence in public places. (Plaques with the Ten Commandments were posted in public schools; the Pledge of Allegiance was recited at the start of each school day, including the "one nation under God" phrase.) Ethical and moral behavior as expressed in Scripture was still acknowledged as the aspirational cultural standard (even if people chose not to adhere to it). Most people at that time may not have revered God, but biblical precepts were, for the most part, acknowledged as beneficial for society.

Back then, challenges to the Christian faith made by sincere seekers or by antagonistic critics were rooted in scientific or evidentiary inquiry. Examples:

- How can you prove that God exists?
- Hasn't the theory of evolution disproved the creation story?
- How can you prove that Jesus actually died after the crucifixion, then came back to life?

But in the twenty-first century, the cultural climate has changed, and the challenges to Christianity are drastically different. Much of the current skepticism concerning Christianity is directed at the *nature* of God. By many people, God is not trusted; his judgment, wisdom, and plans for humanity are suspect. This change of opinion toward God is reflected in the current questions and criticisms of Christianity. Gone are the evidentiary and scientific issues; now the inquiries are couched in terms of social justice, morality, and ethics, such as these:

- If God is all-powerful, why does he allow evil to exist?
- Why does God insist that there is only one way for salvation?
- Why doesn't the all-powerful God alleviate suffering for those who are starving, crippled, or enslaved by poverty?

Maybe the best example of the current attitude toward God is reflected in the question of this chapter: "If God is loving, how could he send anyone to hell?" Implicit in that question is the attitude that (1) sending people to hell is unfair or unjust, and (2) a loving God wouldn't do such a thing, so (3) God might be on the wrong side of this issue.

Don't assume that all Christians resolved this "If God loves . . . why hell?" quandary before they accepted Christ. Like the college students and eighty-year-old guy we mentioned at the start of this chapter, even a few leading theologians and Bible scholars remain befuddled by this question. The famous clergyman John Stott (1921–2011) fell into that category, as he confessed,

> Emotionally, I find the concept [of hell] intolerable and do not understand how people can live with it without either cauterizing their feelings or cracking under the strain.[2]

If you yourself wonder about this question, you've got plenty of company. As Stott's statement suggests, no one has a problem with ascribing a loving nature to God; they just find the juxtaposition of God's love and hell to be irreconcilable. Bottom line: They'd like to keep God's love and just get the hell out of there.

Not all Christians are baffled and bewildered by this question. Many find an explanation clearly presented in the Bible. But the answer isn't readily apparent without an understanding of the biblical doctrines of

• God's holiness,
• humanity's sinfulness, and
• Christ's sacrifice.

Along with the topic of hell, those doctrines have undergone a relatively rapid makeover during the last several decades. This happened in the culture at large and in many *churches* in particular. As a consequence, the Bible doctrines that your grandparents knew have been rebranded to suit this postmodern era. We can't explain the Bible's answer to "If God loves . . . why hell?" without first explaining what you may not even yet realize.

Hell Rebranded: How It Lost Its Popularity

We don't mean "popularity" in the sense of being well liked or enjoyed. (Most people *know* about hell, but nobody ever wants to go there. It's a lot like Fresno.) But for about nineteen centuries, hell was *popular* in the sense that it was a favored topic in the commentary of the Christian faith. It was the stuff of fire-and-brimstone sermons, and it was an essential part of the doctrines of mainstream Christianity.

But by the end of the twentieth century, a funny thing happened: Hell fell out of the public discourse (except as a swear word), and it became a seldom-mentioned topic in churches:

- "Hell disappeared. No one noticed," or at least that was the title of the 1985 report by Professor Martin Marty, a religious historian from the University of Chicago. His research showed that over the preceding eighty years, scholarly theological journals contained not a single article focused on the doctrine of hell.[3]
- By 2002, the phenomenon of the hell's "disappearance" was headline news. The *Los Angeles Times* ran a front-page story, "Hold the Fire and Brimstone," reporting that "hell is being frozen out" as the mention of hell from the pulpit was at an all-time low in churches across America. Citing a May 2001 Gallup poll showing 71 percent adults nationwide still believed in hell, the reporters concluded that "hell is far from dead," but people just don't want to hear about it. The article quoted a pastor from Orange County, California as saying, "[Hell] isn't sexy enough anymore."[4] (In response to which we are compelled to ask, "When was hell ever sexy?")

QUESTIONS FOR REFLECTION AND DISCUSSION

- What's your take on hell? Would you prefer not to think about it?
- If you regularly attend church, can you remember the last time you heard a sermon devoted to that subject?

Sin Rebranded: How It Moved from Notoriety to Obscurity

As just discussed, many pastors and other believers are trying to market Christianity in a postmodern culture—one that emphasizes tolerance and abhors judgment. They deal with hell by avoiding the topic. But the doctrine of sin is more troublesome because it is mentioned with alarming frequency and clarity in the Bible: Every human being has sinned (Romans 3:23); the penalty for our sins is death (Romans 6:23); salvation through Jesus Christ is offered, but it demands repentance from our sins (Acts 3:19). Because the accusation of sin and a demand for repentance are perceived by many pastors to be offensive to the ears of postmodern church audiences, the sin stuff is downplayed in many churches. One seminary professor (quoted in the *Los Angeles Times* article previously mentioned) explained why:

> It is just too negative. Churches are under enormous pressure to be consumer-oriented. Churches today feel the need to be appealing rather than demanding.[5]

Many churches offer a type of "pop evangelism" that waters down—or eliminates—essential biblical doctrine. Pastor and Bible scholar John MacArthur decries those who try to morph biblical doctrines, such as sin, into a concept that fits the cultural model of tolerance, all in an effort to make the Bible sound cheerful to unchurched people:

> They oppose any emphasis on negative biblical truths like sin, hell, the wrath of God, human depravity. . . . Some have even argued that negative themes like those need to be totally eliminated from the evangelical repertoire. Such ideas have an unwholesome, primitive sound, they say—especially in an enlightened postmodern generation where self-esteem, inclusivism, and positive thinking are embraced as high virtues.[6]

QUESTIONS FOR DISCUSSION AND REFLECTION

- In an attempt to avoid offending you, many pastors intentionally omit the very information that explains the answer to the "If God is loving . . . why hell?" question. Do the topics of sin and hell offend you?

- Would you be offended if the topics of sin and hell were omitted from a sermon repertoire simply because they might be perceived as offensive?

God Rebranded: How He Was Reconfigured for the Sake of Political Correctness

Let's face it, the Bible reveals that God isn't politically correct. He's far from it. As a result, Western secular culture has gone in the opposite direction of what the Bible teaches. While the current culture embraces religious pluralism (the philosophy that differing religious views should each be considered as equally valid), the Bible says that Jesus is the only way to God (John 14:6). While society wants all of us to be tolerant of others' conduct and attitudes, the Bible teaches that God has a moral code that is applicable to all, and any violation in thought or deed is sinful (1 John 3:4).

In an attempt to keep God acceptable to the culture, many preachers have chosen to downplay the personality traits of God that are culturally unacceptable (e.g., wrath, judgment, righteousness, holiness). Instead of presenting a complete profile of God, they focus on a certain singular personality trait of God that is socially acceptable and politically correct: *love*. Nobody will have a complaint about a God who is all love and nothing but love.

But there is a big problem with such a one-dimensional god: It is not the God that the Bible describes. God is multidimensional, and you can't understand any single attribute without reference to the others. No single attribute can operate to the exclusion of the others. Theologian Geerhardus Vos has written about the error of focusing solely on God's attribute of love. His premise on this subject has been summarized as follows:

> While God's love is revealed to be his fundamental attribute, it is defined by his other attributes as well. It is quite possible to "overemphasize this one side of truth as to bring into neglect other

exceedingly important principles and demands of Christianity."
... This would lead to a loss of theological "equilibrium" and
balance. In the specific case of the love of God, it often leads to an
unscriptural sentimentalism whereby God's love becomes a form
of indulgence incompatible with his hatred of sin.[7]

QUESTIONS FOR REFLECTION AND DISCUSSION

- Is there an aspect of God's character that you are uncomfortable with?
- If Vos is correct, how might that trait be impacted by God's love, and vice versa?

Yourself Rebranded: How We Have Elevated Ourselves in Our Own Minds

It is our humble (and probably correct) opinion that as a culture,
we have a pretty high estimation of ourselves. But you don't need to
take our word for it. Let's go to the universally recognized authority
on all cultural subjects, UrbanDictionary.com. According to that
website, the top definition for the dominant age demographic in
our society—millennial—is as follows:

> Born between 1982 and 1994 this generation is something special,
> cause Mom and Dad and their 5th grade teacher Mrs. Winotsky
> told them so. Plus they have a whole shelf of participation trophies
> sitting at home so it has to be true.[8]

How did we get to be so self-absorbed? People who are sociology experts suggest that the emphasis on self-esteem has played
a large part:

- The psychological examination of self-esteem gained momentum in 1969 when Nathaniel Branden published *The Psychology of Self-Esteem*. Branden asserted that self-esteem was the single most important facet of a person, placing the highest value on "that supreme expression of selfishness and self-assertiveness which consists of holding [one's] self-esteem as his highest value and most exalted concern."[9]

- Following Branden's treatise, efforts to achieve positive self-esteem moved from the psychiatrist's couch into the general populous. In an August 2007 article for *New York* magazine, journalist Po Bronson warned that excessive praise by parents could be counterproductive. He cited a survey by Columbia University that found 85 percent of American parents think it's important to tell their kids that they're smart (not just regular smart, but far-above-average smart).[10] But if 85 percent of the kids are above average, doesn't that mean that their group is just the new average?

- Moving from the home to the classroom, British journalist Melanie Phillips wrote an article titled "Everybody Wins and All Must Have Prizes." She attributes the collapse of educational systems on cultural and moral relativism, doctrines that hold that no values can be judged to be any better or worse than those of another person. If any and every answer is acceptable, then no one ever has a wrong answer.

Alas, the latest pronouncement from those in charge of our exam system is truly beyond satire. Their new idea for boosting examination success is to abolish the very idea of failure, along with the difference between the right and the wrong answer to a question.[11]

QUESTIONS FOR REFLECTION AND DISCUSSION

- Do you agree that there is an overemphasis on self-esteem in our culture?
- Does it have any impact on how we might confront the "If God is loving . . . why hell?" question?

The Consequence of All This Rebranding: How Our Perspective May Be Skewed

Now that we have reviewed the derivation of society's present impression of hell, sin, God, and our own self-esteem, let's examine the effect of it all.

From a human perspective, God has lost his street cred

Before all of this rebranding kicked into high gear (back in what was the VHS era, to give you a point of reference), there was a popular Christian slogan:

God said it. I believe it. That settles it for me.

But now, things are different. If people have an opinion that doesn't match up with the biblical position, they feel no reason to automatically abandon their viewpoint; to their way of thinking, their stand on a theological topic isn't automatically invalid simply because God has spoken to the contrary. For them, the contemporary version of that now-outdated Christian slogan has perhaps morphed into something like this:

God said it. I'm not persuaded. And I remain highly skeptical.

This is especially true when dealing with the "If God is loving . . . why hell?" question. Many people consider God's "hellish" paradigm as being unfair, unjust, and immoral. And if you feel that way, why shouldn't you?

- Even if you have been attending church, you probably haven't heard any explanation or rationale for the existence of hell.
- On the rare chance that "sin" was mentioned in a sermon, it was probably treated lightly, and you weren't made to feel bad about it.

90

- You've got a gut instinct that the whole sin/hell system is out of whack. You might readily admit that you are not a theologian, but you are confident in your feeling that God needs to rethink *his* strategy on this issue.

If that is you, whether you are a Christian or not, please realize that we can understand how you reached that conclusion. But without intending to be presumptuous, may we suggest that your real objection is not the concept of sin or hell, but rather the issue of the *proportionality of the penalty*. In our discussions with many people on this subject, we find that most of them have no difficulty with these concepts:

- Some conduct could qualify as sin, and sin deserves punishment.
- *Really* bad people (e.g., Adolf Hitler, Osama bin Laden, Jeffrey Dahmer) deserve to be *really* punished. Maybe an eternity in hell is suitable punishment for *them*.
- But for people who are basically good, law-abiding citizens, the prospect of everlasting torture in hell is a supreme overreaction on God's part. No one would tolerate a father beating his teenage daughter for violating her curfew by thirty minutes. So why should we tolerate God sentencing that girl to eternal damnation for the same act (which might technically constitute a "sin")?[12]
- And to bring it down to a personal level, *you* probably believe yourself to be basically good, and the thought that *you* might spend eternity in hell for the offense of not "accepting Jesus" probably seems to be extremely excessive punishment over a matter of your personal preference.

So you see, it isn't really a rejection of the notion of sin or hell per se. Rather, we are repulsed by the *proportionality* with which God imposes the penalty of hell. Bottom line: We struggle with the "If God is loving . . . why hell?" question because, from our human perspective, we feel that God is unfair in his judgment and punishment as applied to most people.

Shouldn't We Examine the Question from God's Perspective?

Earlier we mentioned that many leading theologians confess to having similar feelings of unfairness with the concept of hell. We quoted John Stott who confessed to feeling queasy with the notion of hell, but he also explained that human feelings are not determinative in these matters.

> But our emotions are a fluctuating, unreliable guide to truth and must not be exalted to the place of supreme authority in determining it. As a committed Evangelical, my question must be—and is—not what does my heart tell me, but what does God's word say.[13]

We understand Stott to be saying that if God exists as the Bible describes him, then our *feelings* about hell and judgment are irrelevant. If God's Word is true, then we are stuck with hell and God's punishment as described in the Bible whether we agree with it or not. And for that reason, it is appropriate that we now turn to see what the Bible teaches in an effort to view the "If God is loving . . . why hell?" question from God's perspective.

At the beginning of this chapter, we stated that the answer to that question isn't readily apparent without an understanding of the biblical doctrines of

- God's holiness,
- humanity's sinfulness, and
- Christ's sacrifice.

It's time to embark on that exploration. As we do so in the following pages, we hope you can—at least for the moment—think outside any "rebranding" to which you previously have been exposed and to which you possibly might currently subscribe.

Authors' Disclaimer

[One of us is a lawyer, so here is the obligatory boilerplate.]

As we undertake to examine biblical passages that address the "If God is loving . . . why hell?" question, we feel no compulsion to persuade or cajole you to a certain conclusion. We interpret our task to be an objective presentation of verses that form the Bible's response to the question. If our writing comes across as dogmatic, that is because we'll be dealing with verses that are unequivocal. We'll do our best to explain what the Bible says on this issue. We respect your personal role in deciding if you accept it, reject it, or remain undecided.

God's Holiness: More Pure Than You Could Ever Imagine

The Bible is very clear about this point: God is holy. Not just partially holy. Not a lot holy. But entirely, wholly holy. In his book *The Holiness of God*, R. C. Sproul captures the concept as he comments on Isaiah 6:3 ("Holy, holy, holy is the Lord Almighty; the whole earth is full of his glory"):

> The Bible says that God is holy, holy, holy. Not that He is merely holy, or even holy, holy. He is holy, holy, holy. The Bible never says that God is love, love, love, or mercy, mercy, mercy, or wrath, wrath, wrath, or justice, justice, justice. It does say that He is holy, holy, holy, the whole earth is full of His glory.[14]

Okay, good to know, but what does it *mean*? God's "holiness" is an overarching term, difficult to explain because it is not inherently shared by humanity. It includes purity, but it is much more than that. Because it is impossible for God to sin, maybe "purity in infinite measure" (nothing morally lacking in his character) gets us closer to the full meaning. Also encompassed in the concept of God's holiness are other attributes that reveal who he is:

- *Righteous*—absolutely free of any sin (Psalm 145:17)
- *Good*—including the sense that he can only do good (Psalm 25:8)
- *Just*—fair and impartial (Isaiah 61:8)
- *Perfect in all his ways* (Psalm 18:30)

The list goes on, but we are sticking to the ones most relevant to this chapter.

God's holiness makes him separate

The full magnitude of God's holiness is incomprehensible to humanity because we have no point of reference to anything comparable. The Old Testament prophet said it succinctly: "No one is like you, Lord" (Jeremiah 10:6). Sproul uses a few more words to express the same thought:

> When the Bible calls God holy it means primarily that God is transcendentally separate. He is so far above and beyond us that He seems almost totally foreign to us.[15]

Sproul hints at the derivation of the word *holiness* when he refers to God being separate. The word *holy* is used more than six hundred times in the Bible, always conveying in some manner the idea of *separation*. In our vernacular, we might say something is "a cut above the rest" because it is so much better—and in that respect, God's holiness makes him "separate" in the sense of being far superior to other things (all of which are greatly inferior).[16] He is not just a cut above other gods or humanity that come in a distant second place; God is separate from anyone and anything else because there is no second place. God has no rivals.

There is another aspect of God's separateness. He is completely and eternally separate and removed from anything and everything that is antithetical to his nature. This refers to sin in all of its dimensions and degrees. As a consequence of God's holiness, he cannot be in the presence of sin; he cannot tolerate it. His wholly holiness cannot abide any evil or wrongdoing, even in the most miniscule degree. And that presents the problem for all of us . . . a problem with eternal consequences.

God's holiness demands that he have priority in our lives

Because of God's holiness, he expects that those who follow him will pursue holiness in their own lives (as much as humans are able). In the Old Testament, when God had chosen the Jews to be his representative nation in a world of pagans, God said to them,

> You are to be holy to me because I, the Lord, am holy, and I have set you apart from the nations to be my own.
>
> Leviticus 20:26 NLT

(You get extra points if you noticed the "set apart" reference that applies to holiness.) This instruction was subsequently applied in the New Testament to all Christians (Jews and Gentiles alike): God's standard of holiness should be at the core of how Christians live (1 Peter 1:16).

The practical application can be explained by the biblical references to idols. "No idols" is big on God's list. In fact, in the list of the Ten Commandments, this prohibition takes up the top two spots: #1: "You must not have any other god but me" (Exodus 20:3 NLT). #2: "You must not make for yourself an idol of any kind or an image of anything in the heavens or on the earth or in the sea . . . for I, the Lord your God, am a jealous God who will not tolerate your affection for any other gods" (Exodus 20:4–5 NLT).

Don't get sidetracked by thinking that idolatry only involves a little carved statue on your fireplace mantel. In Bible parlance, an idol is anything that you worship, and anything that preoccupies your time, energy, or thoughts. God doesn't want your worship of other things to displace the priority that he should have in your life. (Remember: God's holiness has no rivals.) Jesus explained it this way when he was asked to identify the greatest of the commandments:

> "'Love the Lord your God with all your heart and with all your soul and with all your mind.' This is the first and greatest commandment."
>
> Matthew 22:37–38

God makes himself and his holiness known to us

God does not play the role of an absentee landlord (a guy who owns the building but can never be found). To the contrary, the Bible declares that God created the cosmos and everything within it (not the least of which is humanity), and that God has embedded evidence of his presence and character all around us. As a result, we have no excuse not to acknowledge his existence and reign. In chapter 4, we presented four philosophical and scientific arguments for the existence of God that require no reference to the Bible, each of which speaks of God revealing himself to humanity. In addition, the Bible declares that God has made himself known to humanity through

- evidence of his glory in the world around us: "The heavens declare the glory of God, and the sky above proclaims his handiwork" (Psalm 19:1 ESV);
- creating a sense of eternity and life-after-death within us: "[God] has planted eternity in the human heart" (Ecclesiastes 3:11 NLT);
- providing to us his Word, the Bible: "You search the Scriptures because you think they give you eternal life. But the Scriptures point to me!" (John 5:39 NLT); and
- sending his Son, Jesus, to earth: "Christ is the visible image of the invisible God" (Colossians 1:15 NLT).

Before we move to a biblical perspective on humanity and its sin, let's review. Here's the Bible's bottom line: The almighty God and Creator of the universe is holy; he has revealed himself and his nature to us, so there is no excuse for our ignorance of his holiness or our disrespect of it.

QUESTION FOR REFLECTION AND DISCUSSION

• What definition would you give for *God's holiness* as the Bible explains it?

Humanity's Sinfulness: More Heinous Than You Could Ever Conceive

Most people consider themselves to be of good moral character because they know many people who are far worse. You can come out looking pretty good when you are compared with those who are vile, depraved, and wicked. But here is the problem: God doesn't evaluate us on a curve. He does make comparisons, but it is always to his own holiness. So all of us—always—fall short of his standard of perfect holiness. The Bible calls this sin, and it can range from violent murder and rape to a far less passionate hand gesture flashed at a driver who cut you off on the freeway.

The Greek word *hamartia* is often used in the New Testament when referring to sin. That Greek term conveys a sense of "missing the mark" (as in archery when the bull's-eye is missed). This is the term used in Romans 3:23 (NLT): "For everyone has sinned; we all fall short of God's glorious standard." But remember, we aren't talking about being a few centimeters to the left of the bull'seye. By God's measurements, we miss the target altogether. No one of us can hit the target of God's holiness.

Don't get distracted by trying to calibrate the severity of sins. On a human level, we like to make those distinctions. Yes, there are sins of commission (doing something wrong) and sins of omissions (our failure to do the right thing); and there are sinful actions as well as sinful thoughts. But God doesn't nitpick among them. To him, any sin is evidence of

- our sinful hearts
- our rebellion against him
- our worship of ourselves

To God, our sinful actions and thoughts don't need to be distinguished from each other. Whatever they are, they all represent an attitude that is antagonistic and hostile toward him.

God sees our hearts as totally depraved

Some of us are better at hiding it than others, but all of us have a sinful nature. It is inherent in us. The Bible says our sin is rooted in our hearts (which has nothing to do with romance or our cardiovascular systems, but instead refers to the center of our emotions and desires). The Bible doesn't give a flattering picture of what God sees in our hearts:

> The heart is deceitful above all things and beyond cure. Who can understand it?
>
> Jeremiah 17:9

> For out of the heart come evil thoughts—murder, adultery, sexual immorality, theft, false testimony, slander.
>
> Matthew 15:19

> For the flesh desires what is contrary to the Spirit, and the Spirit what is contrary to the flesh.
>
> Galatians 5:17

God considers our sin as volitional rebellion against him

As discussed above, God has revealed his presence and holiness to humanity through multiple sources. When we choose to sin, rather than love God with all our heart, soul, and mind, we are making a definite choice to reject him. In other words, we are rebelling against the principles that he, the almighty Holy God, has decreed. As his creations, we are defying our Creator. He finds our revolt to be revolting:

> They are darkened in their understanding and separated from the life of God because of the ignorance that is in them due to the hardening of their hearts.
>
> Ephesians 4:18

> Everyone who sins breaks the law; in fact, sin is lawlessness.
>
> 1 John 3:4

> The mind governed by the flesh is hostile to God; it does not submit to God's law, nor can it do so.
>
> Romans 8:7

God sees our worship of ourselves as idolatry

Remember commandments #1 and #2? God decrees that we should not let our love for anything else displace him from the first-place priority he deserves in our lives. God considers these commandments to be broken when we are living for ourselves. That happens when we do not give God a place of top priority in our lives. Instead, we let the "idols" of our life consume and dictate our lifestyle. These idols are different and self-styled for each of us. Maybe our "god" is

- materialism
- success, power, or prestige
- sexual pleasure and personal enjoyment
- education
- sports and entertainment
- family
- occupation
- charitable work (including being busy at church)

When we are the center of our world, we live for ourselves. Regardless of what form it takes, the "idols" in our lives consume our thoughts, energy, and motivation. The holy God is pushed aside. We might consider it trivial, but God considers it sin. Because he is a righteous and just God, our sin of rebellion and idolatry deserves a punishment appropriate for our offense against the almighty God. The God of infinite fairness has decreed that the penalty for sin is spiritual death:

> The wages of sin is death.
>
> Romans 6:23

In God's paradigm, death is the appropriate penalty for our defiance in the face of his holiness. Romans 6:23 is not speaking of physical death (which is our first death); it is referring to a spiritual death sentence of eternity in hell.

> But the cowardly, the unbelieving, the vile, the murderers, the sexually immoral, those who practice magic arts, the idolaters and all liars—they will be consigned to the fiery lake of burning sulfur. This is the second death.
>
> Revelation 21:8

QUESTIONS FOR REFLECTION AND DISCUSSION

- From the Bible's point of view, explain the dichotomy between God's holiness and humanity's sinfulness. Within the context of your answer, is hell an acceptable penalty for humanity's sin?

Christ's Sacrifice: More Loving Than You Could Ever Comprehend

The Bible never directly addresses the "If God is loving . . . why hell?" question. It doesn't have to. The way the Bible explains it, there is no reason to ask why God sends people to hell. The answer is obvious: God is holy; His created beings have renounced and rejected him by living for themselves; this offense against God is blatant sin justly deserving the punishment of an eternity in hell. Enough said.

But in the context of humanity's wretched sinfulness, there is a different question that deserves an answer: "Because God is so holy and humanity is so sinful, why would God spare anyone from the penalty of hell that they deserve?"

And this is where we come full circle to the subject of God's love.

> This is how much God loved the world: He gave his Son, his one and only Son. And this is why: so that no one need be destroyed; by believing in him, anyone can have a whole and lasting life. God didn't go to all the trouble of sending his Son merely to point an accusing finger, telling the world how bad it was. He came to help, to put the world right again. Anyone who trusts in him is acquitted; anyone who refuses to trust him has long since been under the death sentence without knowing it. And why? Because of that person's failure to believe in the one-of-a-kind Son of God when introduced to him.
>
> John 3:16–18 THE MESSAGE

No sinful human could pay the penalty for another sinful human. Every person deserves that second death in hell for his or her own sin. So it took the death of the perfect, holy, sinless Son of God to pay the penalty for our sins.

> God made him who had no sin to be sin for us, so that in him we might become the righteousness of God.
>
> 2 Corinthians 5:21

Jesus died in our place. In God's paradigm, innocent blood had to be shed to cover the penalty. It is the blood of Jesus Christ that "cleanses us from sin" (1 John 1:7). This substitutionary death (Christ taking the punishment for our sin) was foreshadowed for centuries before it happened. Lambs (spotless and without blemish) had been sacrificed daily at the temple in Jerusalem in a ceremony for temporary forgiveness of sins. Then along came Jesus: the one who was called "the Lamb of God who takes away the sin of the world" (John 1:29), the one who died on the cross as the once-and-for-all sacrifice for all of the sins of all of humanity for all time. Consider the magnitude of God's gift of salvation:

- We did not deserve to be saved. It is a gift of God's grace.
- The gift came at great expense: the painfully agonizing crucifixion of Jesus Christ on the cross.
- God saves us in our sinful condition. God does not require you to clean up your act as a precondition to accepting his gift of salvation.
- God's salvation is a universal offer, open to everyone: Jew and Gentile; male and female; no age restrictions; no criminal record check; no drug test; rich or poor; slave or free; intelligent and not so much so; every nationality and every ethnicity.
- There is nothing we can contribute to the salvation process. It is a free gift. It is not "because of works of righteousness we had done, but because of his mercy" (Titus 3:5).

We close this chapter by repeating the more appropriate question that should be asked when viewing the subject of hell from God's perspective:

Question: Because God is so holy and humanity is so sinful, why would God spare anyone from the penalty of hell that they deserve?

Answer: Because of his great love, God is not willing that anyone should perish; he wants everyone to repent of their sins (2 Peter 3:9). He desires that we would be in an intimate relationship with him for eternity (John 14:3). And to prove it, he allowed his Son to be crucified and pay the penalty for our sin (John 3:16).

The reality of hell does not diminish God's love; it demonstrates it.

7

Is Hell a Divine Torture Chamber?

Introduction

The BBC television series *Sherlock* is a modern-day retelling of Sir Arthur Conan Doyle's classic detective stories. At one point in the series, Holmes has a dream in which he visits his archenemy, James Moriarty, in hell.

For Moriarty, hell appears to be solitary confinement in an insane asylum where he is the only patient. He is wearing a straitjacket, chained to the wall of a tiny round underground room with padded walls and no doors or windows. A divine torture chamber? Maybe not. And these fictional conditions do not compare to those actually suffered by Louis Zamperini, the American POW who was held captive and tortured in a WWII Japanese prison camp (whose story was told in the movie *Unbroken*). But for Moriarty, it is *his* hell.

During a viewing of that episode of *Sherlock* with friends and fellow *Sherlock* lovers, a long conversation was ignited about the nature of hell itself. The conversation wasn't transcribed (an oversight on our part), but the comments went something like this:

> "I think hell is probably very similar to that. Absolute loneliness and no freedom."

"But doesn't the Bible say it's a lake of fire or something?"

"The Bible certainly doesn't seem to paint it as a very pretty place. Or at least the church never has, that's for sure. But it's difficult to imagine a place of constant torture. Even though sin is a big deal."

"Maybe it's our own personal hell. Like Moriarty. Maybe hell is whatever would drive us most nuts."

"If that's the case, then for me hell is definitely a Walmart on the Saturday before Christmas. "

◼ ▓ ◼

Hell . . . a divine torture chamber? Now, how could anyone ever get that impression? Well, maybe from the Bible's description of the judgment that befalls everyone who fails to accept God's offer of salvation—descriptions found in verses like these:

. . . thrown outside, into the darkness.

Matthew 8:12

. . . throw them into the blazing furnace, where there will be weeping and gnashing of teeth.

Matthew 13:42

. . . the eternal fire . . .

Matthew 25:41

. . . eternal punishment . . .

Matthew 25:46

If you do not remain in me, you are like a branch that is thrown away and withers; such branches are picked up, thrown into the fire and burned.

John 15:6

. . . God's wrath . . .

Romans 2:5

. . . punished with everlasting destruction and shut out from the presence of the Lord.

2 Thessalonians 1:9

Blackest darkness is reserved for them.

2 Peter 2:17

When he opened the Abyss, smoke rose from it like the smoke from a gigantic furnace.

Revelation 9:2

. . . God's fury, which has been poured full strength into the cup of his wrath. They will be tormented with burning sulfur. . . . And the smoke of their torment will rise for ever and ever.

Revelation 14:10–11

Anyone whose name was not found written in the book of life was thrown into the lake of fire.

Revelation 20:15

QUESTIONS FOR REFLECTION AND DISCUSSION

• What is your initial reaction to that list?
• Figurative or literal? What do you think? Why?
• Quick. Give your gut reaction: Is hell a divine torture chamber?

What Hell Are We Talking About?

The Bible uses several different terms for what we refer to as *hell*.

• In the Old Testament's original language of Hebrew, *Sheol* is used to describe "the place of the dead" or "the place of departed souls/spirits." The Greek word used in the New Testament for the same meaning is *Hades*. Scriptures in the New Testament convey the idea that Sheol/Hades is a temporary place for unsaved souls—after mortal death but before the final resurrection and judgment. Meanwhile, souls of the saved go directly into the presence of God (2 Corinthians 5:8; Philippians 1:23), the part of Sheol called "heaven" or "paradise" (Luke 23:43).

- Another Greek word in the New Testament, *Gehenna*, is used for hell. *Gehenna* is derived from the Hebrew word *gehinnom*, meaning "Valley of Hinnon." The Valley of Hinnon was located south of Jersalem where some ancient Israelites sacrificed children in a fire offering to the Canaanite's pagan god Molech (2 Chronicles 28:3). The valley carried a despicable reputation thereafter. Later called Gehenna Valley, it was a place where the corpses of criminals and animal carcasses were dumped with the refuse of the city. Historians report that there were often small fires burning constantly in this trash heap. Because of the mental imagery that accompanied it, *Gehenna* was a term often used by Jesus, in a figurative sense, when he was speaking of a place of everlasting destruction, in verses that translate the word as "hell" (e.g., Matthew 5:28; 10:28).

- *Lake of fire* is a term mentioned only in the book of Revelation (9:20; 20:10, 20:14–15). This is the big boy, the place of everlasting punishment for all the unsaved and for Satan and his demons (Matthew 25:41).

Importantly, without ever suggesting a geographic or spatial location, the references by Jesus to hell were always as a literal sphere.

What Is Hell? The Answer You'll Get Depends on Whom You Ask

Surprisingly, there appears to be very broad agreement among Bible scholars about the actual existence of hell. But there is almost equal disagreement about the *nature* of hell (What is it like? Who ends up going there? Is it for eternity or a shorter duration?)

Douglas J. Moo, a New Testament professor at Wheaton College, believes that the disputes and arguments among Christians on the many aspects of hell and judgment can be condensed into two basic issues:

> The New Testament clearly teaches and everywhere assumes that after death God will punish in "hell" those who refuse to trust in Christ in this life. But evangelical Christians disagree over two matters: the *nature* of punishment in hell, and the *duration* of the punishment.[1]

We think Moo's classifications will help us drill down on the "Is hell a divine torture chamber?" question. But before we go there, we want to review the three most popular views of hell among Christians. The limited space in this book (and the limited knowledge in our brains) prohibits us from giving all of the nuances and variations of each view. Our intent is to review the basic principles of each view and to highlight the main points of difference among them.

Traditionalism

This is the hell that you've heard so much about. Traditionalism follows the historical orthodox view of hell to which most Christians adhere (even though some of them struggle with it, as we discussed in chapter 6). In looking for a concise definition of this view, we like the definition used by theologian R. C. Sproul: "Hell, then, is an eternity before the righteous, ever-burning wrath of God, a suffering torment from which there is no escape and no relief."[2] But that description is so succinct that it leaves off what is implied: Hell is the appropriate punishment for all those who reject God's offer of salvation to avoid the punishment. In addition to the elements of eternality and suffering, this view includes other key components:

- Everyone has an immortal spirit that lives on in a conscious state for eternity after their physical death.

- Everyone will live for eternity either in the presence of God (heaven) or separated from God (hell).

- Your eternal destination is determined by the choice you make during your lifetime. You either associate your identity in Christ (making him the central focus of your life), or you reject salvation through Christ and find your identity and purpose elsewhere.

- Hell is final and irreversible. After physical death, there is no second chance to change your mind.

By its detractors (the proponents of the two views discussed below), traditionalism is often called "eternal conscious torment," or simply the ECT view. That label is not incorrect, and the detractors prefer this terminology as a way of contrasting their views of hell (which contain little or no suffering or punishment). Traditionalists are certainly up-front about the everlasting torment and agony in their view, but they are quick to point out that the horror of hell is actually a demonstration of God's love. (We suspect you are rolling your eyes at the last sentence. If not, you probably didn't read it closely enough. But read on; we think this reasoning by the traditionalists makes sense.)

Here's how traditionalists read the Bible. God does not delight in people being in hell. In his love for humanity, God wants everyone to be spared from it, so much so that he allowed his sinless son, Jesus, to be tortured and crucified upon the cross, so that his death could pay the penalty for the sin of all people. In a spiritual sense that no one can comprehend, that pain, agony and horror Christ suffered on the cross was magnified and intensified by the weight of the sins of all humanity. Traditionalists point to the Scriptures declaring that Christ endured the pain of the eternal suffering that we deserved in hell so that we could be spared from it and be freed to spend eternity in God's presence. The Traditionalists contend that it is impossible to understand the depth of Christ's love for us unless we know the horror of the penalty of hell that he voluntarily endured for us.

Annihilationism

Annihilationism is a Christian belief that holds to the position that God annihilates unsaved sinners at death (or at the judgment day, or after a "proportionate" time in hell). Whatever day it is, when it comes . . . *zap*, and you're outta here. Disintegrated. Dissolved. Melted like the Wicked Witch of the West being doused with a bucket of water. "This sounds harsh," you say. "But it is just the opposite," says the annihilationist. If you were an unsaved sinner, which would you rather endure following your earthly demise: suffering punishment for eternity, or being instantly decomposed?

With respect to "saved" sinners, annihilationism follows the traditional biblical view that after death they go on to celebrate living with God for eternity. For this reason, sometimes a slight variation of annihilationism is referred to as "conditional immortality" or "conditionalism," the *condition* being that humans are only *potentially* immortal; you gain immortality if and when you become a Christian during your lifetime.

Annihilationism has always been a minority view, but it is gaining in popularity. (You can understand why unsaved people prefer this view instead of the traditionalist position of everlasting agony.) But of course, the rise in the popularity of this view is from Christians, many of whom are relieved to have an interpretation of the Bible that gives a more satisfactory result on one of Christianity's hot-button issues. As we discussed in chapter 6, a contemporary trend in Christianity downplays the holiness and judgment of God, for the sake of taking a more singular focus on his loving nature. With hell being politically incorrect (what with its judgment, damnation, and all), annihilationism has solved the problem by finding God's love so great as to obviate the need for hell. Proponents of annihilationism posit that immediate annihilation is more compatible with the notion of a loving God.

We are not suggesting that annihilationists have thrown out the Bible and made stuff up. Their camp includes sincere Christians with a desire for biblical scholarship (just like the traditionalists). However, the annihilationists read certain verses in Scripture to reform hell from the "everlasting" traditional view to an instantaneous destruction, which makes the penalty for sin more proportional to our sense of justice:

- The annihilationists exegete the word *death* in hell and judgment verses to mean instantaneous disintegration. In their view, when Romans 6:23 says "The wages of sin is death," it means a one-and-done extinction—nothing prolonged, nothing eternal.

- Similarly, when end-times verses refer to *destruction*, this is not a prolonged, unending suffering in hell. Rather, *destruction* means a terminal point in time.

- Regarding references to *eternal* (as in the Matthew 25:46 description of "eternal punishment"), annihilationists claim that such passages only mean punishment at a time in the future—in "the age to come" and does not mean "everlasting."

The exegesis of the annihilationists is exclusive to their own camp. As traditionalist Douglas Moo points out, *destruction* in end-times texts does not necessarily mean "cease to exist," but can instead mean "cease to be what one once was,"[3] as in "the situation of a person or object that has lost the essence of its nature or function."[4] As you might expect, traditionalists believe that a term like *eternal* actually means "everlasting." They cite verses like Matthew 25:46, where Jesus says, "[The wicked] will go away to eternal punishment, but the righteous to eternal life."

Everyone agrees that *eternal life* means "everlasting life" (as in "whoever believes in Him should not perish but have everlasting life" from John 3:16 NKJV). Consequently, the traditionalists argue that Jesus also intends that *eternal punishment* means "everlasting punishment." Annihilationism has nothing "everlasting" about it.

Universalism

This is the view that says *everyone* will be saved. While this view has been around at least since the third century AD, it had very little traction until the 1800s and is now adopted by some prominent scholars and many others. The view is growing in acceptance, but it is still very much a minority position. The doctrine of universalism has been characterized as follows:

> At the heart of this perspective is the belief that, given enough time, everybody will turn to God and find themselves in the joy and peace of God's presence. The love of God will melt every hard heart, and even the most "depraved sinners" will eventually give up their resistance and turn to God.[5]

Under this view, Christians still go directly to heaven. And the unsaved still go to hell, but only temporarily. So it is okay if you don't become a Christ-follower during your lifetime, because in your postmortem eternity, you've got a second chance (or chances) to respond to God's love. In the meantime, you are stuck in hell with all of its concomitant agony. As theology professor J. I. Packer explains universalists' view of hell:

> It is a rough reality, a house of correction as well as a place of conversion; it is the milieu in which the perverse and deluded come to their senses, and to that end it needs to be dreadful, as Jesus in particular stressed that it is. It is a kind of purgatory for those—that is, the totally Christless ones—whom official Roman Catholicism would not admit to purgatory.[6]

There are hybrid positions under the umbrella of universalism:[7]

- *Non-Christian universalists* (more often called pluralists) believe that any and all religions are equally effective as to

111

salvation—other faiths besides Christianity can get you to heaven.

- *Hopeful universalists* follow traditional biblical doctrine of heaven and hell, but it is their hope that God won't be such a stickler on the rules, like the verse that says, "Turn to me now, while there is time" (Joel 2:12 NLT). They are hoping he'll eventually save everyone.

- *Dogmatic universalists* are sticking with the Jesus-is-the-only-way-to-be saved doctrine, but they believe the Bible clearly teaches that everyone eventually gets to heaven.

Traditionalists find the Bible's references to *everlasting* judgment, and the absence of any "second chance" verses, to be objections that the universalists can't explain away.

QUESTIONS FOR REFLECTION AND DISCUSSION

- Are you drawn to one of these three views more than the other two? Why?
- Can you critique each view, mentioning strengths and weaknesses of each position?
- How important is biblical support in determining the validity of a view of hell?

We didn't forget that we promised to explore the two categories of disagreement among Christians on the subject of hell (as mentioned by Douglas Moo). Now that we have reviewed traditionalism, annihilationism, and universalism, our job is a little easier, as you will see.

The *Nature* of the Punishment in Hell: It Still Depends on Whom You Ask

Remember that list of Bible verses at the beginning of this chapter? Those descriptions portray hell as being horrific. In fact, they are so dreadful, one has to wonder if the descriptions are only metaphorical instead of literal.

In the traditional view, some hold tight to the position that the biblical descriptions are literal and mean exactly what they say. But it seems that the majority position is that the biblical descriptions of hell are metaphorical. This later group points to the fact that the Bible gives conflicting descriptions: Hell is a "place of darkness," yet it is a place of "fire" (2 Peter 1:17 and Matthew 25:41). As both fire and darkness together seem incompatible, contemporary scholars read the biblical descriptions of hell as metaphors. But don't get too excited about that. Just because the terms are metaphors doesn't mean that the underlying concept is fanciful or nonexistent. The same scholars believe that in metaphors used by Jesus and others there was no terminology sufficient to describe the degree of the horrors in hell. In other words, the reality of hell is probably even worse then the metaphors.

For annihilationists, the "Figurative or literal?" question also applies. Remember, under their reading of Scripture, it is all about actual destruction (which they take very literally). But for the universalists, this becomes an almost irrelevant question. Everyone goes to heaven and everyone escapes the *everlasting* part of punishment. For those who need a little time in "interim" hell to change their minds about God, their punishment will be literal but equally temporary.

The *Duration* of the Punishment in Hell: This, Too, Depends on Whom You Ask

This is going to be easy:

- Traditionalism: Everlasting means everlasting.
- Annihilationsim: *Poof!* and you are destroyed.
- Universalism: Only as long as it takes you to change your mind.

A Picture of Hell as Painted by Jesus

If you are going to ask for information about hell, we think Jesus is the definitive go-to source on the subject. His most comprehensive description of hell is found in the parable of the rich man and Lazarus in Luke 16:19–31. Before we dissect that passage, we need to insert a preface about parables.

The parables of Jesus are fictional stories, but that does not mean that they are void of truth. To the contrary, Jesus used these metaphorical stories to illustrate truth to those who wanted to hear it, and to obscure the message from those who were opposed to it. As John MacArthur has said, "The parables are tools in which Jesus taught and defended the truth."[8] The points of the parables are always consistent with gospel truth, but the reader should not get distracted with the narrative details that are nonessentials to the overall truths and which are not intended to be an extension of the analogy. (For example, in the parable you are about to read, don't get distracted by angels carrying Lazarus or Lazarus dipping his finger in water. The point to notice is that Lazarus is in heaven and the rich man is in Hades. And for your sake, we are using a translation that refers to "Abraham's side" instead of other translations that refer to "Abraham's bosom.") Finally, as MacArthur reminds us, Jesus "was not inviting His hearers to interpret the stories any way they liked."[9]

The parable you are about to read is the third in a series of three parables that Jesus presented, all dealing with the same principle: The decisions you make during your lifetime impact your destiny after death. Think on that principle as you read the parable.

The rich man and Lazarus

"There was a rich man who was dressed in purple and fine linen and lived in luxury every day. At his gate was laid a beggar named Lazarus, covered with sores and longing to eat what fell from the rich man's table. Even the dogs came and licked his sores.

"The time came when the beggar died and the angels carried him to Abraham's side. The rich man also died and was buried. In

Hades, where he was in torment, he looked up and saw Abraham far away, with Lazarus by his side. So he called to him, 'Father Abraham, have pity on me and send Lazarus to dip the tip of his finger in water and cool my tongue, because I am in agony in this fire.'

"But Abraham replied, 'Son, remember that in your lifetime you received your good things, while Lazarus received bad things, but now he is comforted here and you are in agony. And besides all this, between us and you a great chasm has been set in place, so that those who want to go from here to you cannot, nor can anyone cross over from there to us.'

"He answered, 'Then I beg you, father, send Lazarus to my family, for I have five brothers. Let him warn them, so that they will not also come to this place of torment.'

"Abraham replied, 'They have Moses and the Prophets; let them listen to them.'

"'No, father Abraham,' he said, 'but if someone from the dead goes to them, they will repent.'

"He said to him, 'If they do not listen to Moses and the Prophets, they will not be convinced even if someone rises from the dead.'"

Luke 16:19–31

What this parable teaches about hell

Here are just a few of the many truths that can be drawn from this parable. We'll begin by talking about the type of life that ends up in hell:

1. *Separation from God in the afterlife is determined by ignoring God during one's lifetime.* What was it about the rich man's life that resulted in his going to Hades after death? It wasn't the fact that he was rich (Abraham was very rich during *his* lifetime). It wasn't that the rich man ignored religious traditions (to the Jewish audience that heard this parable, it was assumed that the rich man participated in the rituals of his Jewish faith). The answer can be found in the description of the rich man and the contrasting description of Lazarus.

The rich man was opulently, extravagantly, excessively wealthy—from the fine linens he wore to the daily luxuries he enjoyed to the palatial estate in which he lived (as evidenced by the gate at which Lazarus lay every day).

Contrast that to the beggar Lazarus. He was starving daily, wishing for just a crumb from that rich man's table. Realize that the rich man personally knew Lazarus (he called him by name in the conversation with Abraham); he probably walked by him every day, never giving Lazarus one of those crumbs; he wouldn't even attend to the open sores on Lazarus' body. The sin of the rich man was having an identity and core values that had nothing to do with God and everything to do with himself. He lived for "today" with no regard for his "eternal tomorrow." He was oblivious to God's passion for loving others.

2. *Heaven and hell exist; they are the only options in the afterlife. They are both eternal and final.* As Abraham told the formerly rich man, there is no crossing over. There is a permanent, irrevocable separation between heaven and hell. There is no end to either of them.

3. *Hell doesn't change the sinful predispositions of the unsaved.* Isn't it fascinating that the former rich man appears to be as pompous and obnoxious as he must have been in life? Now in Hades, he is still bossing people around. He wants Lazarus to be his servant (telling Abraham to send Lazarus to Hades with water, and to send Lazarus as a messenger to the rich man's brothers). Notice that the rich man never expresses a word of regret or repentance. In fact, he doesn't even ask to be released from Hades. The self-centered, self-absorbed identity he had in life has not dissipated. Just as James Moriarty had his own form of hell, the rich man's hell may be the fact that he has to live with himself for eternity. Theologian C. S. Lewis made a similar comment about the nature of hell:

116

Christianity asserts that we are going to go on forever and that must either be true or false. Now there are a great many things that wouldn't be worth bothering about if I was only going to live eighty years or so, but I had better bother about if I am going to go on living forever. Perhaps my bad temper or my jealousy are getting worse so gradually that the increase in my lifetime will not be very noticeable but it might be absolute hell in a million years. In fact, if Christianity is true, hell is precisely the correct technical term for it. Hell begins with a grumbling mood, always complaining, always blaming others, but you are still distinct from it. You may even criticize it in yourself and wish you could stop it. But there may come a day when you can no longer. Then there will be no you left to criticize the mood or to even enjoy it, but just the grumble itself going on and on forever like a machine. It is not a question of God "sending us" to hell. In each of us there is something growing, which will BE hell unless it is nipped in the bud.[10]

If you think that living with your sinful self for eternity may not be such a bad punishment, think again. Jesus clearly stated that the rich man felt the torment and agony of his hell.

4. *God does not delight in people being in hell, but he allows them to suffer the consequences of their own choices.* There are those who think that God is punitive and cruel, happy to sentence people to an eternity in hell. This parable displays the opposite attitude. Despite the continued arrogance of the rich man, notice that Abraham calls him son. That is a term of endearment. There is not a shred of animosity, cruelty, or retribution coming from Abraham. Instead, he softly explains that the rich man is getting what he brought on himself.

5. *If the Bible doesn't persuade you of your need for Christ, nothing will.* The rich man asks that Lazarus go back to earth and warn his brothers. He is sure that seeing someone raised from the dead will be sufficient proof and motivation for his brothers to repent. But Abraham doesn't agree. Abraham says that God's story is clearly explained in the Scriptures, and if God's Word doesn't convince them, nothing will. Don't miss the irony in the story. At the time it was told, Jesus knew that he soon would be crucified and resurrected. He would be the story of a dead man coming back to life that is included in the writings of the New Testament. That is a resurrection story that all of us must consider.

We will let you come to your own conclusions about the nature and duration of hell. But if you look to Jesus for information, the parable of Lazarus and the rich man indicates that hell is real, eternal, and torturous.

QUESTIONS FOR REFLECTION AND DISCUSSION

- Do you agree that these truths are apparent in the parable? Do you see others?
- How does the parable sync with the respective views of traditionalists, annihilationists, and universalists?
- Is hell a divine torture chamber?

8

How Do You Get into Heaven?

Introduction

It was a typical Monday morning, and Colin, a youth pastor, drove to church to begin another week of ministry. As he turned into the parking lot, something seemed amiss. There were no cars anywhere to be seen. The associate pastor's motorcycle and the students' bikes that were often chained to the outside bike rack were gone. Colin scratched his head and mumbled, "It's Monday, right?"

He stepped from his car and meandered onto the church campus. The church's small coffee bar, where high schoolers religiously gathered for a morning cup of joe, was vacant. The preschool playground? Eerily silent. Colin unlocked the building and found every office, room, and hallway abandoned. *What is going on?* he pondered as his anxiety rose.

Finally, a colleague stepped out of the silence. Colin spotted him and yelled like a lost seaman spotting land, "Dave! Thank God! I was beginning to think the rapture happened!"

After a mild case of confusion then a robust round of laughter, Dave said, "I don't think it was the rapture, man. I'm pretty sure it's just Memorial Day. Everyone's off today." Colin had obviously missed the memo. His youth pastor's sense of humor quickly kicked in and he joked, "I should have known. There's no way the rapture happened if you're still here. But I was beginning to seriously dread explaining to our high schoolers that their youth pastor was left behind and I must be clueless about how to get to heaven!"

■ ■ ■

A national poll shows that the vast majority of Americans believe in heaven and hell. "In all, 76% believe that Heaven exists, while nearly the same proportion said that there is such a thing as Hell (71%)." That's not shocking to us. What caught our attention is this: "Nearly two-thirds of Americans (64%) believe they will go to Heaven" but "just one-half of 1% expect to go to Hell upon their death."[1] In summary, the vast majority of us assume we have a reservation to God's eternal party.

In his book *Heaven,* Randy Alcorn tells the story of a singer who sang at the wedding of a very wealthy couple. After the ceremony, a select group of guests went to the penthouse floor to enjoy fine food, wine, dancing, and celebration. When the singer reached the door, the maître d' could not find her name on the list. Surprised, she told the man that she was the singer who had just performed in the wedding ceremony! The maître d's response was firm: "It doesn't matter who you are or what you did. Without your name in the book you cannot attend the banquet." And just like that, the singer and her date were sent away. As it turned out, the woman had failed to RSVP before the event because she assumed she was already on the list.[2]

The story poignantly illustrates the nature of our hearts today. If God is handing out trophies, we believe we deserve one. After all, we haven't murdered anyone lately, and everyone agrees that Hitler was a very bad guy. That's good enough to earn us eternal bliss with a perfect God, right?

There was once a time when everyone assumed the opposite. People instinctively knew they were unworthy of a holy God. Today is quite different. We prefer to think of God as our sweet old grandpa who still works the admission booth at the county fair. If we just give him a smile and a wink, he'll chuckle and let us (and all our friends) in without paying admission. But is that assumption correct? How *do* we gain access to heaven?

QUESTIONS FOR REFLECTION AND DISCUSSION

- If you were asked, "Are you going to heaven?" how would you respond? Why?
- What if you were asked, "How do you know you're not going to hell?" How would you respond and why?
- If you believe you're going to heaven, why do you think your name is on that "list"? And how did it get there?

What Gets Us In?

Before we wrestle with the nearly irresistible question of who is going to heaven, it's vital we remember two things. First, God loves us with an incredible, otherworldly, unfathomable kind of love. Second, the Christian life is not solely concerned with entrance to heaven. That would be like going to a friend's birthday party simply because you want cake. Dessert is a sweet perk, but the true reason to attend is because you have a relationship with the birthday boy or girl. Too many people, churches, and preachers focus on the gifts and not the Giver when, at the end of the day, God himself is the point. It is him alone who loves us, created us, and redeemed us. Life with him includes access to heaven, but we will miss out big time if heaven alone is our aim.

That said, the important question remains: What gets us into heaven? As it turns out, the Sunday school answer (Jesus!) is correct. The gateway to heaven is not a *what*, but a *who*.

I am the way

Take a close read of John 14:1–14. Jesus tells his disciples that he is going to be with God the Father, and he will prepare a place for his followers there. We don't know about you, but if we stood face-to-face with Jesus and learned his plan to take us to God, we would be more excited than a hound dog at a steak dinner.

But his words confused his faithful pack of disciples. He said, "You know the way to the place where I am going" (verse 4). Thomas, a disciple who (like you!) is not afraid of asking questions, piped up: "Lord, we don't know where you are going, so how can we know the way?" (verse 5). Jesus' oft-quoted reply is central to Scripture. He said, "I am the way and the truth and the life. No one comes to the Father except through me" (verse 6).

In one short sentence Jesus answers our question "How do we get to heaven?" But did you notice that Jesus' words to Thomas were not directional, but personal? The disciples were curious about how to get to heaven and see God, but instead of a step-by-step guidebook, Jesus gave himself.

Imagine a stranger, with a car full of hungry kids, pulling up to ask you for directions to McDonald's. What if instead of pointing her to the fast-food joint, you held out your arms, and said, "*I am* the hamburger." We have a sinking suspicion that she would whisper, "Buckle up, kids," hammer the gas, and drive away as fast as possible. Why? Because you would have sounded *crazy*! Yet that's exactly what Jesus did. Thomas and the gang were looking for Jesus' turn-by-turn navigation for knowing God and getting to heaven (just like us). But instead of instruction, Jesus offers an introduction. Jesus did *not* say, "I *know* the way, I *know* the truth, and I *know* how to have life." He personified the instruction and said, "I *am* the way and the truth and the life."

The answer to our question is not position, perfection, a prayer, or a plan. It's a person. Without Jesus we can neither hope to know God nor spend a perfect eternity with him. But in Jesus, we have both.

Knowing Jesus

When it comes to Bible passages about our eternal standing with God, we must admit that Jesus said some stuff that is not easy to read. In the Gospel of Matthew, Jesus' words about true followers and false imitations are pointed and convicting and cause a bit of humble trembling.

> "Not everyone who calls out to me, 'Lord! Lord!' will enter the Kingdom of Heaven. Only those who actually do the will of my Father in heaven will enter. On judgment day many will say to me, 'Lord! Lord! We prophesied in your name and cast out demons in your name and performed many miracles in your name.' But I will reply, 'I never knew you. Get away from me, you who break God's laws.'"
>
> Matthew 7:21–23 NLT

It's difficult to admit, but Jesus' words make it clear: Knowing him and seeing heaven require more than simply attending church on Christmas and Easter or saying an acceptance prayer in grade school (though both can be where it all begins). Jesus taught that heaven is a blissful reward for those who *do the will of the Father* and who *know* Jesus.

Two important questions are born out of this passage. Do we seek to accomplish what God wants, and do we have a real, current, intimate relationship with Jesus? We don't presume to be God with the ability and right to see into anyone else's hearts, but this is apparent: If we answer those questions with a no, we must wonder if we are indeed a Christian and if we will someday experience heaven.

The second challenging but important passage is from Matthew 25. In it, Jesus says,

> "But when the Son of Man comes in his glory, and all the angels with him, then he will sit upon his glorious throne. All the nations will be gathered in his presence, and he will separate the people as a shepherd separates the sheep from the goats. He will place the sheep at his right hand and the goats at his left.

"Then the King will say to those on his right, 'Come, you who are blessed by my Father, inherit the Kingdom prepared for you from the creation of the world. For I was hungry, and you fed me. I was thirsty, and you gave me a drink. I was a stranger, and you invited me into your home. I was naked, and you gave me clothing. I was sick, and you cared for me. I was in prison, and you visited me.'

"Then these righteous ones will reply, 'Lord, when did we ever see you hungry and feed you? Or thirsty and give you something to drink? Or a stranger and show you hospitality? Or naked and give you clothing? When did we ever see you sick or in prison and visit you?'

"And the King will say, 'I tell you the truth, when you did it to one of the least of these my brothers and sisters, you were doing it to me!'

"Then the King will turn to those on the left and say, 'Away with you, you cursed ones, into the eternal fire prepared for the devil and his demons. For I was hungry, and you didn't feed me. I was thirsty, and you didn't give me a drink. I was a stranger, and you didn't invite me into your home. I was naked, and you didn't give me clothing. I was sick and in prison, and you didn't visit me.'

"Then they will reply, 'Lord, when did we ever see you hungry or thirsty or a stranger or naked or sick or in prison, and not help you?'

"And he will answer, 'I tell you the truth, when you refused to help the least of these my brothers and sisters, you were refusing to help me.'

"And they will go away into eternal punishment, but the righteous will go into eternal life."

Matthew 25:31–46 NLT

Convicting, right? Of course! And we see two things here that are crucial to our understanding of what it means to know Jesus rather than to just know about him.

First, those who know God's heart do what is best for their neighbors, particularly "the least of these." It's clear here that people who love God love people because God loves people. When you discover what makes God's heart tick, do you do those things, motivated by gratitude for what he's done for you? That in itself is a glimpse of heaven.

Second, pay close attention to the farm animals here. Have you ever noticed how Jesus—the Good Shepherd—refers to us as his sheep? (See John 10.) It's no compliment. Sheep are stupid, weak, and prone to wander away from their Shepherd and into great danger. Sound familiar? It describes us perfectly. Yet according to Jesus it is the sheep who "follow him because they know his voice" (John 10:4) and who will "go to eternal life" (Matthew 25:46).

Have you detected a theme? Heaven is a place full of people who *know* the Good Shepherd, not simply know about him. Thankfully it's God who initiates that relationship (more on that later). But first, if Jesus gets us in, what keeps us out?

QUESTIONS FOR REFLECTION AND DISCUSSION

- Why is Jesus' answer to Thomas' question difficult to grasp?
- What are the tangible differences between knowing Jesus and merely knowing about Jesus? Which describes you? Why?
- Why do we prefer for God to give us a list of directions rather than pointing to Jesus?

What Keeps Us Out?

If the one-word answer to "Who gets us into heaven?" is Jesus, then the one-word answer to "What keeps us *out* of heaven?" is sin (cue the dark, depressing music here). We don't mind chatting about Jesus, but we *hate* talking about sin. It makes most of us so nervous or angry that we break out in hives. Well, friends, grab some antihistamine because we're about to jump right in! If we truly want to wrestle with questions about heaven and hell, Jesus, and eternal salvation, we can no longer avoid it. When it comes to life and afterlife with God, talking about sin is a necessary evil.

What is sin anyway?

"What *is* sin?" is a good question because we can't be expected to address it if we don't even know what it is.

One of the most helpful explanations of sin is given by Cornelius Plantinga in *Not the Way It's Supposed to Be*. He calls sin the "vandalism of shalom."[3] But to grasp that definition, we need a biblical understanding of the Hebrew word *shalom*. Here is Plantinga's thoughtful explanation:

> The webbing together of God, humans, and all creation in justice, fulfillment, and delight is what the Hebrew prophets called *shalom*. We call it peace, but it means far more than mere peace of mind or a cease-fire between enemies. In the Bible, shalom means *universal flourishing, wholeness, and delight*—a rich state of affairs in which natural needs are satisfied and natural gifts fruitfully employed, a state of affairs that inspires joyful wonder as its Creator and Savior opens doors and welcomes the creatures in whom he delights. Shalom, in other words, is the way things ought to be.[4]

Take a moment to imagine the "way things ought to be." What do you see? Now turn on your local or national news. Does your imagination match the news feed? Probably not.

It doesn't take anyone very long to recognize that the world is broken. *Shalom*—"universal flourishing, wholeness, and delight"—has been marred by a dark and terrible graffiti: sin. "Sin is blamable human vandalism of these great realities."[5] Or as the candid English writer Francis Spufford put it, sin is "the human propensity to [mess] things up."[6] Only he didn't use the word "mess." In short, sin is what's wrong with the world.

But this vandalism is not restricted to violent crime and impersonal headlines. It's in all of us. We've tried to brainwash ourselves into believing sin has no impact. But the truth sobers us, because it does. Even in seemingly innocuous situations our personal sin violates shalom. And asking a few questions helps us to see, and wrestle with, this truth.

126

- Are lies (even little white ones) meaningless? Or do they break trust in marriages, friendships, business, and government?
- Is greed just the cousin of ambition? Or does greed breed poverty, more lies, greater selfishness, and less contentment with what we already have?
- Is gossip simply idle chatter? Or does rumor spreading and defamation crack community, degrade innocent people, and incubate pride?
- Is pride simply healthy self-esteem? Or is pride the fuel for prejudice and racism and the ignoring of those in need?
- Is pornography only a private pleasure rush? Or does porn objectify real people and contribute to human trafficking, sexual abuse, disease, and addiction, and radically warp God's good design for sexuality?

We could ask the same kinds of questions for a slew of our favorite sins, and we would continue to discover that sin erodes shalom, destroying the way we know things ought to be.

Why Does Sin Keep Us from God and Out of Heaven?

So sin is real. It's a violation of all that is good and works against our mutual thriving, fulfillment, and joy as families, friends, communities, and a world. That part seems clear. But why is it such a big deal to God?

For and against

The primary reason God is against sin is because he is *for* shalom! And because he is so good, he will not tolerate those who are hell-bent on destroying shalom for the people he created and loves. Christians ought to oppose sin, but far too often our judgmental rants against "sinners" (as if we are not sinners ourselves) pigeonhole us as people who fight what is bad but never celebrate what is good. And that, our friends, is not representative of God. God *delights* in what he has designed and loves it when it works as designed. He longs for us to thrive in love, joy, and peace with him, each other, and the world. So when we vandalize shalom through sin, God's heart breaks, and we see that his passion for good is balanced with his fierce opposition to evil.

Insult to injury

Imagine if an architect friend of ours designed a beautiful new home perfectly suited for our family—and did it for *free*. Now imagine our first response to the thoughtful design was, "Hmm. Looks okay. But give us the plans and we'll design something much, much better." Not only would it be foolish (because we are *not* architects!), it would be personally insulting to the designer. Ditto for God, only on a *much* grander scale. God designed us and this world to work perfectly together, so our arrogant rebellion against his plans and preference for our own destroys shalom *and* spits in the face of the One who designed it for us. In essence, our sin-filled declaration is "We can do it better because we're smarter than you, God!" Why, then, would he *want* to spend eternity, in a place he made, with anyone who thought that kingdom, and therefore the King, weren't all that great?

Holy, holy, holy

The last reason sin keeps us out of relationship with God, and therefore out of heaven, is because of who God is. He is holy.

- The prophet Isaiah referred to God as "the high and exalted One . . . who lives forever, whose name is holy" (Isaiah 57:15).
- Peter (the disciple of Jesus) wrote, "Just as he who called you is holy, so be holy in all you do; for it is written: 'Be holy as I am holy'" (1 Peter 1:15–16).

128

- And in the vision of heaven that Jesus gave to John, the beings who worshiped God said, "Holy, holy, holy, is the Lord God Almighty, who was and is and is to come" (Revelation 4:8 ESV).

Holy is not a word we use much anymore (unless it precedes an expletive). In the Bible's original languages, the word *holy* is packed with meaning. Something holy is sacred and morally perfect, set apart and awe-inspiring. For God to be holy means he is the one perfectly pure being, completely set apart and worthy of great reverence and awe. God himself, like *shalom*, is the way things are supposed to be: right, good, spotless, amazing.

A friend of ours recently bought a car, and before it was a week old someone carelessly backed into it and gouged a huge scratch and dent into his new pride and joy. What was perfection before was now marred, and it needed to be made right. Everyone knows there are two ways to make it right: (1) The party who caused the damage is held responsible, and (2) the car needs to be restored. That is a rudimentary example. But it holds true for situations with much higher stakes.

God is perfect, and he created the perfect environment in which humankind could thrive physically, emotionally, relationally, and spiritually. But our sin trashed that ideal reality and was a personal affront to the holy God who created it. It makes sense, then, that those who busted it should be responsible for making it right, and God's perfect, divine nature—his holiness—requires it.

QUESTIONS FOR REFLECTION AND DISCUSSION

- If a friend asked you to define and describe sin, how would you answer?
- Do you think sin is as big a deal as God makes it and we describe it? Why or why not?
- If sin is such a big deal, why is it so rampant? Why don't we simply stop it?

> • Why do you think sin keeps us out of heaven? Are there any
> reasons we left out?

Who and What Can Make It Right?

Now we have reached an impasse. We've seen that knowing and obeying Jesus is the way. But we've also recognized that sin is the roadblock to knowing God and experiencing heaven. Because of God's holiness, it would be wrong for him to simply wink at sin and the damage it causes to the people he loves. So now what? We have been diagnosed, but how are we cured? We know the answer is "Jesus," but let's wrap up this chapter by talking about how Jesus actually cures our sin disease.

The Bible shows us that out of God's great love, Jesus came and is the perfect substitution we sinners so desperately need to reconcile with our Holy Father. And most of us are familiar with Jesus' substitution for us in death. "He died on the cross for our sins," as many an evangelical would say. But in equal importance was Jesus' perfect life. Here's how it's expressed in Scripture:

> God put the wrong on him who never did anything wrong, so we
> could be put right with God.
>
> 2 Corinthians 5:21 THE MESSAGE

> Christ suffered for our sins once for all time. He never sinned, but
> he died for sinners to bring you safely home to God.
>
> 1 Peter 3:18 NLT

> You know that he appeared in order to take away sins; and in Him
> there is no sin.
>
> 1 John 3:5 ESV

> This High Priest of ours understands our weaknesses, for he faced
> all of the same testings we do, yet he did not sin.
>
> Hebrews 4:15 NLT

In regard to his substitution in death, Jesus said it best: "I am the good shepherd. The good shepherd lays down his life for the sheep" (John 10:11). Jesus' dear friend Peter realized what Jesus had done and wrote, "He personally carried our sins in his body on the cross so that we can be dead to sin and live for what is right. By his wounds you are healed" (1 Peter 2:24 NLT).

As we discovered above, sin causes damage that must be paid for. Death is the right and good punishment for something as destructive as sin. But instead of death for sinners, Jesus took the hit in our place. He was separated from God, and on our behalf died the brutal death sinners deserve *even though he did not sin at all*. He was the substitute for us in death.

That leads us to the other way Jesus stood as our substitute: by his life. Take a look at the verses above again, and you will see the Bible's witness to Jesus' sinlessness. Phrases like "in him there is no sin" and "he faced all of the same testings we do, yet he did not sin" remind us that Jesus lived the only life fully acceptable to our Holy God, because he was perfect. One hundred percent pure. He obeyed perfectly and was fully in step with God and fully contributed to God's *shalom*. And because he lived on our behalf, God graciously poured out *on us* the favor, acceptance, and love that is due Jesus. Jesus died as a substitute for our death, and lived as the substitute for our life!

What's Our Part?

Jesus has done it all (thank God!). So what's our role in knowing God and going to heaven? Have you heard the phrase "We are saved by grace alone"? It's an important part of the Christian faith and originates from verses like this in Ephesians 2:

> But because of his great love for us, God, who is rich in mercy, made us alive with Christ even when we were dead in transgressions—*it is by grace you have been saved*. And God raised us up with Christ and seated us with him in the heavenly realms in Christ Jesus, in

order that in the coming ages he might show the incomparable riches of his grace, expressed in his kindness to us in Christ Jesus. *For it is by grace you have been saved,* through faith—and this is not from yourselves, it is the gift of God.

Ephesians 2:4–8 NIV, emphasis ours

God so loves us that he took full responsibility for initiating the process necessary to restore us, save us from sin, and make it possible to live with him forever in heaven. That undeserved gift—given by God for nothing we did, can do, or will ever do—is grace. And at the end of the day, it is God—by graciously giving himself in Jesus Christ—who makes the way for us to get into heaven. We are just the grateful recipients of his unbelievable gift.

Here's the reason grace alone (Ephesians 2) and knowing and obeying Jesus (Matthew 7 and 25) work together. The moment we fully realize who Jesus is and what he has done, God's love sparks in us a desire to know and obey him. The natural response is to recognize his love, confess our sin, and give our lives fully to him. And that leads us to knowing him and loving others in ways we never have before. John wrote it simply and eloquently in 1 John 4:19, "We love because he first loved us." It is that love that leads to a real—and eternal—experience of God.

QUESTIONS FOR REFLECTION AND DISCUSSION

- How would you describe your relationship with Jesus right now?
- What is more important to you, knowing Jesus or getting into heaven?
- If heaven didn't exist, would you still want to know and follow Jesus? Why or why not?
- Have you ever fully trusted Jesus to be the King of your life? If so, take a few minutes to write out your story.
- If not, do you know how much Jesus loves you, and do you sense him calling you to trust him with all of your life? How do you want to respond?

9

What Will Heaven Be Like?

Introduction

In a recent preaching class, a seminary student preached out of the following well-known passage from Hebrews, one of the last books of the New Testament.

> Therefore, since we are surrounded by such a great cloud of witnesses, let us throw off everything that hinders and the sin that so easily entangles. And let us run with perseverance the race marked out for us, fixing our eyes on Jesus, the pioneer and perfecter of faith.
>
> Hebrews 12:1–2

She began her sermon by engaging our imaginations. She asked us to pretend we were runners competing to win the race in a huge stadium with every seat filled by a cheering crowd. With each hurdle jumped and every lap completed we felt lighter and quicker, and we focused intently on Jesus, who set the pace ahead of us. Each time he looked over his shoulder, we felt encouraged to press on. Each time we heard the crowd roar as we neared the finish line, our adrenaline rushed.

The race, she explained, was life. Jesus was the perfect athlete, pulling us on by his grace and example. And the cheering crowds, she said, were all the Christian saints who had gone on before us. They were "a great cloud of witnesses" that looked down from heaven to see our progress and encourage us on toward the prize.

It was a moving introduction. And though her sermon was not about heaven, I could not shake the illustration from my mind. Several classmates and I grappled with her manifestation of heaven. We asked, "Is it possible that those Christians who have died before us can see us? Do they cheer us on? Is this why athletes point to the sky when they score touchdowns and hit homeruns? Is grandma up there watching?"

The questions flowed freely, but in the end, we found ourselves wrestling with just one: "Exactly what will heaven be like?"

We're just going to say it right up front. There are no good movies about heaven and the afterlife. None. A quick look at the Internet Movie Database's selection of "40 Movies Dealing in Some Way with the Afterlife"[1] (that title alone should tell you something) proves our point. In alphabetical order, here are ten of the best Hollywood has to offer:

Beetlejuice (1988)—Tim Burton's imaginative take on what happens when you die, or more correctly, when Alec Baldwin and Geena Davis die.

Field of Dreams (1989)—Kevin Costner plays baseball with dead major leaguers.

Ghost (1990)—Patrick Swayze dies and connects to Demi Moore through amateur medium Whoopi Goldberg.

Heaven Can Wait (1978)—A Los Angeles Rams quarterback played by Warren Beatty returns to life in the body of a recently murdered millionaire.

Heaven Is for Real (2014)—The only "Christian" movie in our list—included because so many Christians read the book on which it is based—stars Greg Kinnear as the father of a boy who has been to heaven and back.

Hereafter (2000)—Directed by Clint Eastwood, a drama about three people who experience death in different ways.

It's a Wonderful Life (1946)—Frank Capra's timeless tale about an angel who helps Jimmy Stewart see what life would have been like if he never existed.

The Lovely Bones (2009)—This Peter Jackson–directed movie centers on a murdered girl who watches her family and murderer from purgatory.

The Sixth Sense (1999)—With one of the greatest surprise endings of all time, this M. Night Shyamalan movie is about (spoiler alert) a boy who communicates with spirits who don't know they're dead.

What Dreams May Come (1998)—After he dies in a car crash, a man played by Robin Williams searches heaven and hell for his wife.

Not exactly the most acclaimed movies in motion picture history, but it's not for lack of trying. Some well-regarded directors have given the afterlife a shot, but nothing they've done has captured the true wonder and grandeur of heaven. But that's not Hollywood's fault. If you were asked to direct a realistic movie about heaven (assuming you had the money and talent to pull it off), how would you approach it?

Go ahead, let your imagination run wild. What would heaven be like in your movie? It's not easy, is it? Despite the best efforts of highly creative people, it's almost impossible to depict in words or images the grandeur of heaven. Even Jesus, who was sent from heaven to live on earth, was skimpy in his description. The bottom line is that we don't know what heaven looks like because we don't have a lot to go on.

- Here's your chance. What would your movie about heaven be like? How would you describe heaven? What kinds of special effects would you use?
- How often do you think about heaven? If you rarely think about it, why? What would it take to get you thinking more about heaven?

What Does the Bible Say About Heaven?

The Bible is very clear about a lot of things, including these four essential truths about God and the way he has related to us:

- The Bible is the highest authority for what a Christian believes.
- Jesus Christ's death on the cross is the only sacrifice that could remove the penalty of sin.
- Only those who trust in Jesus Christ alone as their Savior receive God's free gift of eternal salvation.
- It is very important for Christians to personally encourage non-Christians to trust Jesus Christ as their Savior.

As for other very important details, such as how the universe got here and how it's going to end, the Bible is less clear. And when it comes to what goes on in the world of the supernatural, where God dwells in heavenly splendor, the Bible can be downright cryptic.

Thankfully, we have the apostle John, who knew Jesus better than anyone. He was one of the three disciples (along with Peter and James) who spent the most time with Jesus. John was at the foot of the cross when Jesus died (John 19:25–27). He was also among the first to see the empty tomb and had at least three encounters with the risen Savior before Jesus ascended into heaven. Besides writing the Gospel that bears his name, John wrote the book of Revelation and three letters to early Christians about how we should live as God's children in this world, waiting for Christ to return (1 John 2:28). When it came to heaven and what that was all about, John was less certain: "What we will be has not yet been made known" (1 John 3:2).

And so it is. God has not given us a detailed picture of what heaven will be like and what our lives will be like when we get there. But he has given us clues in this world about what life will be like in the next. It's not a complete blueprint, but the descriptions we do have are compelling enough to engage our imaginations and create an appetite for a place where every longing of the soul is satisfied.

On the night he was betrayed, Jesus gave us some of the clues in a room filled with his disciples. John was among them, and he was the only biographer to record these words about the place where Jesus was going:

> "Do not let your hearts be troubled. You believe in God; believe also in me. My Father's house has many rooms; if that were not so, would I have told you that I am going there to prepare a place for you? And if I go and prepare a place for you, I will come back and take you to be with me that you also may be where I am."
>
> John 14:1–3

Many years after the young John heard these words, he wrote a description about that "place," a description given to him in a series of visions.

> Then I saw "a new heaven and a new earth," for the first heaven and the first earth had passed away, and there was no longer any sea. I saw the Holy City, the new Jerusalem, coming down out of heaven from God, prepared as a bride beautifully dressed for her husband. And I heard a loud voice from the throne saying, "Look! God's dwelling place is now among the people, and he will dwell with them. They will be his people, and God himself will be with them and be their God. 'He will wipe every tear from their eyes. There will be no more death' or mourning or crying or pain, for the old order of things has passed away."
>
> Revelation 21:1–4

Later in this same chapter of Revelation, John lists some physical characteristics of heaven, but in this passage the description is glorious enough. Heaven will be a place where every wrong will be righted, every evil wiped out, all sorrow eliminated, and death obliterated. The "old order" of this present world will be replaced by a new perfect order. All things will become new as the children of God enjoy their heavenly Father and his wonderful Son forever.

We could end this chapter right here and say that we have explained enough about heaven to spark your imagination and satisfy your soul. But you want to know more, and that's the way it should be. You want your money's worth, and we want to give it to you. So here are seven questions about heaven. We'll do our best to fill in the blanks, as long as you keep in mind that most of what we will experience in heaven remains a mystery.

QUESTIONS FOR REFLECTION AND DISCUSSION

- Why don't we have more information about heaven in the Bible?
- Reflect on John 14:1–3. Why would the disciples' hearts have been "troubled"? How does this assurance of Jesus about heaven calm troubled hearts today?
- How will God's presence in heaven be different from his presence in your life right now?

Question 1: "What will be our first impressions when we get to heaven?"

A few years ago my (Stan's) family drove to the Grand Canyon for the first time. It was dark when we arrived, so we checked into a small cabin, one of several operated by the National Park Service, and went to bed. I woke up before the rest of the family and decided to go outside and look around. After a short walk, a clearing in the trees revealed a sight I was unprepared for. It was the Grand Canyon, spread out far and wide and deep before me in a way that dwarfed my mental images of what I thought it would be like.

For the previous eight hours, I had been sleeping in a cozy cabin, unaware that our rented abode was less than fifty yards from the rim of this spectacular place. Now in the light of morning, I gazed with wonder at the astonishing vista before me. And I actually wondered, *Is this what it will be like on that first morning in heaven, only a thousand times more amazing?*

Perhaps, but only because we are expecting heaven to unfold only through our outer senses—sight, hearing, and touch. As incredible as the physical manifestation will surely be, however, these first impressions will no doubt be surpassed by an awareness of something much more profound and deeply abiding. Author Scot McKnight puts it this way:

> If God is just and heaven is about God making all things right, the "first hour" in heaven will be a time when all things are first made right . . . with God, with ourselves, and with one another. Heaven will not be heaven until that first hour of realization awakens us to God's deep truths about God, ourselves, and our fellow humans. In the first hour in heaven our innermost life will be as clear to God and others as glass.[2]

It's difficult to imagine what that will be like. Frankly, the thought of it is beyond our comprehension. But there's more! After we experience the ultimate and permanent healing God has for us, we will become aware of what is missing in heaven. R. C. Sproul lists ten things: tears, sorrow, death, pain, darkness, ungodly people, sin, temples, the sun or moon, and the curse from Adam's sin.[3]

But there's more! In that first hour in heaven we will notice something inexplicably wonderful: the presence of God. Wayne Grudem, in his *Systematic Theology*, puts it this way:

> More important than our freedom from pain and sorrow and physical suffering, and more important than reigning over God's kingdom—more important by far than any of these will be the fact that we will be in the presence of God and enjoying unhindered fellowship with him.[4]

Question 2: "Who will be there?"

When Christians consider a question like this, they usually think of other people—family, friends, famous Christians from history, etc. But isn't it likely that all of our fellow Christians in God's family will be subsumed by the presence of Jesus, also known as the Lamb of God? In John's vision, he saw innumerable angels circling the throne with the living creatures and the elders of heaven saying in a loud voice, "Worthy is the Lamb, who was slain, to receive power and wealth and wisdom and strength and honor and glory and praise!" (Revelation 5:12).

Right now most of us are focused on what it takes to get to heaven. If we're being completely honest, we may even feel a wee bit smug, knowing we're in, when other really bad people (murderers, rapists, terrorists, lovers of disco music) won't be in heaven bringing down the celestial property values. But that's the wrong perspective. When we preoccupy ourselves with what it takes to get into heaven, it inevitably leads to comparisons, and we end up missing the whole point of heaven.

Heaven is not about us. We did nothing to earn our ticket. Getting into heaven is totally by God's grace, not by anything we have done or could do (Ephesians 2:8–9). Even more, it's because of God's grace found in Jesus. He is the reason we are going to heaven, and he will be the reason we are there. McKnight writes, "Heaven is designed for Jesus and all those who want to be connected to him. Heaven is not about what we do, but about who Jesus is."[5]

Question 3: "Will heaven be anything like the world we live in now?"

This is actually a very good question. Many people believe heaven is a place "up there" in the clouds where angels fly around playing harps. Others think heaven isn't a real place at all, but rather a state of mind. They're wrong. According to the Bible, heaven is a *place*. Jesus said as much when he promised, "I go to prepare a place for you" (John 14:2 ESV). In fact, heaven is a place that exists now, because heaven is where God dwells. Heaven is where Jesus ascended to in full view of his disciples (Acts 1:9).

So is heaven "up there" in the sky, in space, somewhere in our universe—or is heaven in another dimension? What we do know is that it will be a "new heaven" replacing the "first heaven" (Revelation 21:1). Even more, the Bible indicates that the new heaven will contain the "new Jerusalem" (verse 2). This is the part of Revelation where you read about heaven having streets paved with gold and gates made of pearls. This is not fairy-tale stuff. It's a literal city, most likely the city Abraham hoped for, "the city with foundations, whose architect and builder is God" (Hebrews 11:10). According to the Bible, this is the city we long for:

> For here we do not have an enduring city, but we are looking for the city that is to come.
>
> Hebrews 13:14

Revelation 21 lists the dimensions of this Holy City as a 1,400-mile cube. These dimensions could be symbolic, showing that heaven would hold all of God's people, but someone with too much time on their hands estimated that 20 billion people could fit into a city this size, with each person having a 75-acre mansion.

But there's more! Besides the new heaven with the new Jerusalem as its capital, there will also be a "new earth" (2 Peter 3:13; Revelation 21:1). For those who struggle with heaven being "out there" rather than "down here," this is great news. The earth you enjoy today, in all its variety and incredible beauty, will be part of heaven, but infinitely more beautiful.

Our home planet is an amazing place, but there are problems. Natural disasters, drought, melting polar ice caps, animal-born diseases, and more are constant threats. It's a jungle out there. The apostle Paul explains why. Just as God's children are waiting for "the glory that will be revealed in us," creation is "groaning as in the pains of childbirth right up to the present time," waiting "to be liberated from its bondage to decay and brought into the freedom and glory of the children of God" (Romans 8:18–22). The new earth will be a liberated and liberating place.

QUESTIONS FOR REFLECTION AND DISCUSSION

- Describe a time when you saw something for the first time that was far greater than your expectations. How did you feel?
- Have you ever thought about your experience in heaven affecting your inner being more than your outer senses? How does this change your appreciation of heaven?
- How will it be possible for us to be aware of the negative things that aren't in heaven, yet not dwell on them, since there will be no more tears?

Question 4: "What about God?"

Will we actually *see* God with physical eyes? This is a tough question to answer, because God is a spirit (John 4:24). According to our earthly, physical laws now, we would not be able to see him. But in heaven it will be a different world with different properties and a whole new reality. Saint Augustine, considered by many to be among the smartest Christians who ever lived, speculates:

> Perhaps God will be known to us and visible to us in the sense that he will be spiritually perceived by each of us in each one of us, perceived in one another, perceived by each in himself; he will be seen in the new heaven and earth, in the whole creation as it then will be; he will be seen in every body by means of bodies, wherever the eyes of the spiritual body are directed with their penetrating gaze.[6]

Question 5: "What will we look like?"

Sometimes the best we can do when we think about heaven is to imagine it will be a place where you can eat all the ice cream you want and never gain weight. That may seem trivial, but it brings up a good point about heaven. Our bodies have flaws and imperfections. All of us struggle with physical challenges. Worst of all, we are all aging, which doesn't make any difference when you're in your twenties. But when you hit fifty, look out. We begin to break down more than a car manufactured in Eastern Europe.

When we get to heaven, we may not look like supermodels and Olympic athletes, but we know this: We are guaranteed a resurrected, glorified body. Paul contrasts our present bodies, which decay and die ("perishable"), to our resurrected bodies ("imperishable"), which will be full of glory and power and will never die. "When the perishable has been clothed with the imperishable, and the mortal with immortality, then the saying that is written will come true: 'Death has been swallowed up in victory'" (1 Corinthians 15:54). All of this is possible because of Jesus, who became "the first of a great harvest" (verse 20 NLT) of those who will be raised to life again. As Randy Alcorn writes, "Of this we can be certain—no matter what we look like, our bodies will please the Lord, ourselves, and others."[7]

Related to the question of what we will look like are two other questions all of us wonder about: "What age will we be in heaven, and will we recognize each other?"

The age question is a legitimate one. I (Stan) had a sister who was stillborn. I know she will be in heaven, but will she be a baby or an adult? What about someone who dies in old age, or whose body has been destroyed? What about those who have been dead long enough for their body to completely decay?

We have two theories to offer. One is a tradition in the Catholic Church, which holds that everyone in heaven will be as they appear at the age of thirty. Thomas Aquinas got a little more specific, saying we will all be thirty-three years old, the same age of Christ when he was crucified and resurrected.

As for recognizing each other, we can only speculate. If we use Jesus as our example, we probably will. In his postresurrection body, Jesus was not recognized at first by Mary Magdalene (John 20:14). The disciples on the road to Emmaus did not know who Jesus was until he opened their eyes (Luke 24:13–32). On the other hand, the disciples who saw Jesus on the shore as they were fishing "knew it was the Lord" (John 21:12).

Question 6: "What will we do in heaven?"

Are you concerned that heaven might be a boring place? Will it be like one long vacation, where you enjoy your time away until the very end, when you get bored and you're ready to go home? Many people believe this is going to be the case in heaven.

There are two problems with this analogy. One, most of us can't imagine being happy and fulfilled doing anything for a long period of time, let alone for eternity. But that's because we don't know what unbroken happiness is like. We can't even imagine it. Two, we can't fathom what it will be like to always be in God's presence. That will be anything but boring.

But there's more! Not only will we be in God's presence, but we will also be able to grow in knowledge and truth. When we get to heaven, we will begin the endless and endlessly fascinating task of exploring, learning, and loving the facets of infinity and the inexhaustible nature of God.

Think about this. In other belief systems, you are less than you were after you die. The materialist says you disappear. The Buddhist says you become one with the cosmos. Hindus believe you are reincarnated (probably as something a lot worse than before). Christianity alone says you become more than you were before you die.

Scot McKnight calls this the heaven promise, which means "our bodies will function right, our social institutions and social forms will be right, and our society will be the way God designed it."[8] Think of your best day ever. Now multiply it by a million and imagine your life in heaven being even more satisfying than that.

And here you thought you were going to be bored.

Before we move to the last question, let's talk about the seminary students in the story at the beginning of this chapter who wonder if the "saints" in heaven (especially grandmas) can see us and cheer us on. Hebrews 12:1–2 seems to indicate this. Reading those verses makes you think of a bunch of athletes competing in an arena cheered on by the crowd. But is that what the writer of Hebrews had in mind? The quick answer is no—for one very simple reason. The Greek word translated as "witnesses" is the origin of the English word *martyr* and therefore refers not to spectators but to the saints in the "faith hall of fame" in the previous chapter. The people listed in Hebrews 11 are witnesses to us of what it takes to run with perseverance, but it's likely they aren't watching us.

If anything, these verses are a reminder that we are the ones who should be watching the witnesses, even as we fix our eyes on Jesus.

Question 7: "What does it mean to have eternal life?"

Just as our increasing knowledge in heaven does not mean we will have *complete* knowledge (only God is omniscient), we won't become infinite like God. Even though we will experience eternal life, we are finite creatures. For us, heaven won't be "timeless." Rather, we will exist in a world of "endless time." There will be a sequence to our lives, our worship, our enjoyment, and our relationships. We will always live in a succession of moments, but those moments will never end.

Here on earth, time is our enemy. Rarely do we have the luxury of time. Instead, we feel its pressure. Every twenty-four hours a new day begins, whether or not we have finished our business from the previous day. Every new week, every new month, and every new year reminds us that time marches on. And ultimately (usually when we least expect it) we run out of time. It's never a pleasant prospect.

In heaven, we will never run out of time. Revelation speaks of a heavenly city where there is no darkness due to the light that comes eternally from the glory of God (Revelation 21:23). But that doesn't mean there will be no time. Even though there is no night, there are days: "On no day will its gates ever be shut, for there will be no night there" (Revelation 21:25). And there are months: "On each side of the river stood the tree of life, bearing twelve crops of fruit, yielding its fruit every month" (Revelation 22:2).

These will be days and months filled with inexpressible joy, because we will see the Lord himself and be with him for eternity. "In the face of God we will see the fulfillment of all the longing we have ever had to know perfect love, peace, and joy, and to know truth and justice, holiness and wisdom, goodness and power, and glory and beauty," writes Grudem.[9] We will experience forever in heaven what we merely taste here on earth. "You will fill me with joy in your presence, with eternal pleasures at your right hand" (Psalm 16:11).

In his book *Letters to Malcolm: Chiefly on Prayer*, C. S. Lewis speculates for all of us what we can only dream about:

> Then the new earth and sky, the same yet not the same as these, will rise in us as we have risen in Christ. And once again, after who knows what aeons of the silence and the dark, the birds will sing and the waters flow, and lights and shadows move across the hills, and the faces of our friends laugh upon us with amazed recognition. Guesses, of course, only guesses. If they are not true, something better will be. For "we know that we shall be made like Him, for we shall see Him as He is."[10]

What will heaven be like? As extraordinary as we can imagine it to be, it will be something much better.

QUESTIONS FOR REFLECTION AND DISCUSSION

- What do you think of the theory that everyone in heaven will be as they appear at the age of thirty? Do you have any theories that are more plausible?
- Speculate for a moment on what it will be like to continue growing in knowledge throughout eternity. How does this change your perception about heaven?
- Why do you think all religions except for Christianity teach that you will be less than you were before you die?

10

How Can I Be Sure About Heaven?

Introduction

Anne's friend Rachel recently asked this question: "Am I going to heaven?"

Anne and Rachel met in AA (Alcoholics Anonymous) only a few weeks after Rachel placed her faith and trust in Jesus. Rachel became a Christian, finding that the "Higher Power" everyone talks about in AA is the same God who came to earth as Jesus, died for our sin, and conquered death by rising from the grave. The God who had helped deliver her from alcoholism is the same God who delivered her from sin. That was two years ago, and friends like Anne were thrilled to see Rachel's life filled with new meaning and purpose, and the beginnings of a healthy and God-centered community.

But recently Rachel fell off the wagon, not just in regard to her alcoholism, but in all of life. She gave in to ever-present temptation, made a string of poor decisions, and was involved again in self-destructive behavior. She stopped moving toward God and began moving away from him.

Anne consulted a pastor and asked him the same question Rachel had asked her: "Is Rachel still going to heaven?" The question, no matter who asks it, is laced with a dozen unspoken ones. "How can we know we are saved?" "How much sin is too much?" "If we fail, are we out of God's grace?" "Did we ever really know God and trust Jesus in the first place?" "Does God let us go, or can we lose our salvation?"

In the end, Anne was hopeful her friend would return to God, turn from her sin with his help, and find safety, hope, and help in a community of other sinners saved by grace. But what she, or any of us, cannot truly know is the state of Rachel's heart and the true nature of her relationship with Jesus. So she wonders, is Rachel going to heaven?

■ ▓ ■

Over the years, we've received thousands of emails from readers who have read our books and reached out with comments and questions. Lots of questions. And we can say without equivocation that the most common question people pose is the one Anne is asking about her friend Rachel: "Is she going to heaven, and how can I be sure?"

Very often, this is the way the question is posed. People generally don't ask this of themselves. They ask it about another person, such as a mother for a wayward son, or someone like Anne for her friend Rachel. That being said, it's a question all Christians have about themselves at one time or another, and there's nothing wrong with it. Just because you have doubts about your "eternal security" doesn't mean you are disappointing God, prompting him to erase your name from the Book of Life because you wonder if your name is written there in the first place.

In this chapter, we're going to approach this question from two perspectives. First, we'll take care of this business of eternal security. We aren't going to try to "prove" to you that it's not possible for someone who has truly been saved by God's grace through faith alone in Christ alone to "lose" their salvation (although we believe that). But we do want to offer some reassurance that you don't have to live under the burden of doubt when it comes to the validity of your faith and what that means for you eternally. Second, we will offer some suggestions for living an eternal kind of life, which we believe is a more important and productive activity than worrying about your eternal security.

Eternally Secure by God's Grace

When talking about how you can know for sure that you're saved, perhaps an analogy will help. Imagine you earned a medical degree and passed all of your boards to qualify for a medical license. You then opened a practice and began seeing patients. Now, what if every time you treated a patient, you first looked at your diploma and checked your certification to make sure you were qualified and licensed to practice medicine? It would be unnecessary, if not obsessive.

As silly as this sounds, isn't that what we sometimes do as Christians? We wake up in a cold sweat at night thinking about heaven, wondering if we're going to be there. So we grab a Bible and read some verses (if we can find them) telling us that our salvation is secure. Of course, it would be nice if there were some kind of diploma on our wall declaring that our salvation is for real (sorry, your perfect Sunday school attendance certificate from the third grade doesn't count), but such a diploma doesn't exist. Diplomas and certificates are given to people who *earn* their degrees or qualify for their accomplishments by meeting certain qualifications.

Where your standing before God is concerned, there's absolutely nothing you can do to earn it. Here's the way Paul explains it: "For it is by grace you have been saved, through faith—and this is not from yourselves, it is the gift of God—not by works, so that no one can boast" (Ephesians 2:8–9).

We've been through this in a previous chapter, but we need to go through it again, because like Rachel, we believe at one time or another that the validity of our salvation depends on our spiritual performance. As a result, we sometimes wonder if we're truly saved. We goof up or fail to live a life that pleases God, and we think our performance—or lack thereof—will disqualify us when it comes to heaven. The truth is, we can never do enough to earn our way to heaven. Mother Teresa couldn't, Billy Graham couldn't, not even Paul the apostle could. He understood that it is by God's *love* for us that God showed us *mercy* and saved us through *grace* by faith in Jesus (Ephesians 2:4). Randy Alcorn writes,

> This gift cannot be worked for, earned, or achieved in any sense. It's not dependent on our merit or effort but solely on Christ's generous and sufficient sacrifice on our behalf. Ultimately, God's greatest gift is himself. We don't just need salvation, we need Jesus the Savior. It is the person, God, who graciously gives us the place, Heaven.[1]

The reason you are eternally secure is because you are eternally secure in Christ, who is the one who is both the gift and the gift giver. Knowing this, his statement about being the Good Shepherd takes on new meaning:

> "My sheep listen to my voice; I know them, and they follow me. I give them eternal life, and they shall never perish; no one will snatch them out of my hand. My Father, who has given them to me, is greater than all; no one can snatch them out of my Father's hand. I and the Father are one."

> John 10:27–30

QUESTIONS FOR REFLECTION AND DISCUSSION

- Describe a time in your life when you wondered if you were truly saved and going to heaven.
- If you were having a cup of coffee with Rachel, and she told you that she doubted her security in Christ because of what she had done, what would you tell her?

Living an Eternal Kind of Life

Grace is truly amazing, but it doesn't exist in isolation. Once you receive it, there needs to be a response. Your performance—or "good works"—do not qualify you for heaven, but don't discount them. Your good works count for something. Following his statement that salvation is by grace alone, Paul makes it clear what our response to God's grace should be: "For we are God's handiwork, created in Christ Jesus to do good works, which God prepared in advance for us to do" (Ephesians 2:10).

For those who respond by faith to God's salvation plan, eternity begins now. That's why it's not enough to simply claim the promise of life in heaven but act as if nothing has changed. Becoming a Christian is not merely an invitation to go to heaven when we die, but also an invitation to follow Christ for the rest of our lives. Following Christ isn't a passive thing. It's an active engagement that involves doing those things God has prepared for us to do.

As Christians, we have a responsibility to live what Dallas Willard calls "an eternal kind of life."[2] Since Jesus is the one who makes this life possible, we need to follow his life and obey his teachings. In other words, we need to become *disciples* of Jesus Christ. This is the most effective way to live now in light of eternity.

This may seem like a tall order, especially for someone like Rachel, who has slipped back into self-destructive behavior after placing her faith and trust in Jesus. Come to think of it, that's a tall order for any of us, because we've all been where Rachel is. But it's not hopeless, as long as we recognize that living a life that pleases God is possible only if we invite him to live his life through ours.

Following Jesus as His Disciple

When we exchange the life we have for the life Jesus offers by trusting in him for our salvation, we take on a new identity, literally becoming a new person. "Therefore, if anyone is in Christ, the new creation has come: The old has gone, the new is here!"

(2 Corinthians 5:17). This doesn't happen through a self-help program or by trying really hard. We need God's help to live an eternal kind of life.

Those who have a new life in Christ must daily depend on God and ask him to give us the desire to actively follow Jesus and learn from him (that's the essence of discipleship). Dallas Willard prefers the term "apprenticeship." He puts it this way: "Our apprenticeship to him means that we live within his word, that is, put his teachings into practice (John 8:31)."³

How do you do this? Here are five dimensions or stages of the eternal kind of life suggested by Willard:⁴

1. *Confidence and reliance upon Jesus.* Relying on Jesus entails living by faith, having "confidence in what we hope for and assurance about what we do not see" (Hebrews 11:1). Faith is a renewable resource. Each day, as we look to God for help, we can count on his steadfast love, faithfulness, and mercies (Lamentations 3:22–23).

2. *Having a desire to be an apprentice of Jesus.* As we follow him and put his teachings into practice, our lives will be integrated into "the glorious world of eternal living." Once again, God will give us the desire to live for him. "For it is God who works in you to will and to act in order to fulfill his good purpose" (Philippians 2:13).

3. *Naturally wanting to obey.* There's an old hymn titled "Trust and Obey." Trusting in Jesus and obeying him go together. In the same night when Jesus promised his disciples that he was going to prepare a place for them, he also said, "If you love me, keep my commands" (John 14:15). Those who love Jesus by doing those things he asks "will be loved by my Father, and I too will love them and show myself to them" (verse 21). "Love of Jesus," writes Willard, "sustains us through the course of discipline and training that makes obedience possible."

4. *Leading a godly life.* The power and love of Jesus gives us "everything we need for a godly life through our knowledge of him who called us by his own glory and goodness" (2 Peter 1:3). Christians sometimes balk at the notion of living holy lives, but that's exactly what apprentices of Jesus do.

> As obedient children, do not confirm to the evil desires you had when you lived in ignorance. But just as he who called you is holy, so be holy in all you do; for it is written: "Be holy, because I am holy."
>
> 1 Peter 1:14–16

This is what it means to live the eternal life. It's not sitting back waiting for heaven. It's being engaged in following Jesus fully. Thankfully, we don't have to do this on our own. Because of what Jesus has done for us, God has given us the ability to lead a godly life. Here's how Peter explains it:

> His divine power has given us everything we need for a godly life through our knowledge of him who called us by his own glory and goodness. Through these he has given us his very great and precious promises, so that through them you may participate in the divine nature, having escaped the corruption in the world caused by evil desires.
>
> For this very reason, make every effort to add to your faith goodness; and to goodness, knowledge; and to knowledge, self-control; and to self-control, perseverance; and to perseverance, godliness; and to godliness, mutual affection; and to mutual affection, love. For if you possess these qualities in increasing measure, they will keep you from being ineffective and unproductive in your knowledge of our Lord Jesus Christ. But whoever does not have them is nearsighted and blind, forgetting that they have been cleansed from their past sins.
>
> Therefore, my brothers and sisters, make every effort to confirm your calling and election. For if you do these things,

you will never stumble, and you will receive a rich welcome into the eternal kingdom of our Lord and Savior Jesus Christ.

2 Peter 1:3–11

5. *Doing good works.* The culmination of the first four dimensions is the good works that we will do when everything else is in place. The astonishing thing is that Jesus promises that they will be even greater than the works he did (John 14:12). "Perhaps we feel baffled and incompetent before this statement," writes Willard. "But let us keep in mind that the world we live in desperately needs such works to be done."

God may not need your good works, but the world does. While we are on this earth, we need to be actively engaged in bringing the light and love of Jesus to a world that desperately needs both. And we can't live as if we have all the time in the world. There needs to be a healthy urgency to our lives. We can't put off what we need to do today.

QUESTIONS FOR REFLECTION AND DISCUSSION

- Reflect on this statement often attributed to Dallas Willard: "Live your life the way Jesus would live your life if he had your life to live." How do you do that?
- Describe a time when you were discouraged at the end of the day, but experienced renewed hope when you looked to the Lord the next morning.
- Review the list of spiritual qualities found in 2 Peter 1:3–11. Picture these as stair steps, beginning with faith at the bottom and love at the top. Why do you think Peter listed them in this order?

Prepare for Later Now

When you make a decision to live an eternal kind of life, you are committing to live your life as a disciple of Jesus, following him, learning from him, and obeying what he said. Yet it's possible to do those good works God planned for you to do, and yet fail to keep something very important in mind. This world is coming to an end.

There is a theme running through Scripture centered on the "day of the Lord." The Old Testament prophets talked about it (Amos 5:18–20; Joel 3:14–16), Jesus talked about it (Matthew 24:36), Paul talked about it (1 Thessalonians 5:2), Peter talked about it (2 Peter 3:10), and John talked about it (Revelation 16:14). There will come a day when God brings this present world to an end and ushers in the world to come.

The Old Testament prophecies concerning the day of the Lord stressed that it could happen at any time. God's justice and judgment are certain, as is his mercy. Although some of these prophecies were fulfilled in particular events—Christ came to earth the first time, and the Holy Spirit was poured out after Jesus ascended into heaven—they will culminate when Jesus comes a second time in final judgment and glory.

The big question, of course, is when will this happen? When is Jesus coming back? As we discussed in chapter 4, from time to time Christians obsess over this question, sometimes getting caught up in setting a date. This occasional obsession is usually fueled by so-called prophetic preachers who take advantage of unusual global events—such as the formation of the state of Israel after World War II, or the threat of world domination by a crazy dictator—to set a date for Christ's return. But those fanatics are easily dismissed precisely because they do something Jesus said couldn't be done, and that's to set a date for his return.

At the other extreme of setting dates is completely ignoring the reality of Christ's return, something C. S. Lewis addresses in a brilliant essay, "The World's Last Night." Lewis reminds us that Jesus' teaching on the subject of his return consists of three propositions: (1) that he will certainly return, (2) that we cannot possibly find out when, (3) and that therefore we must always be ready for him.[5]

It is precisely because we cannot predict the moment when Christ will return that we must always be ready, not with fear, but with awareness. Lewis uses the phrase "take it into account." Imagine you are seventy years old. You aren't panicked by the reality that you will likely live no more than another twenty years, but you are wise to take that into account as you plan the rest of your life. It would be foolish to plan something that would take twenty years to complete, but it would be wise to get your house in order by making a will.

Lewis then draws a clever analogy between the end of your own life and the day of the Lord: "What death is to each man, the second coming is to the whole human race."[6] The world may not end tomorrow (although that is always a possibility), but it will most certainly end. In light of eternity, the world is "precarious, temporary, provisional."[7]

With that in mind, we want to leave you with three ways to keep the future of the world and of your own life in perspective. There's no need to panic, but you need to "take it into account." According to Scripture, you need to be *ready*, *wise*, and *watchful*.[8]

- *Be ready.* You never know what's going to happen in the world or in your life. As the Bible says,

  > Why, you do not even know what will happen tomorrow. What is your life? You are a mist that appears for a little while and then vanishes.
  >
  > James 4:14

  Even if Jesus does not return in your lifetime, he will in effect return for you when you die. You don't know when that day will come, and you need to be ready.

- *Be wise.* Don't fear the future, but take into account how to live for God right now, doing those things God has prepared for you to do.

Be very careful, then, how you live—not as unwise but as wise, making the most of every opportunity, because the days are evil. Therefore do not be foolish, but understand what the Lord's will is.

Ephesians 5:15–17

- *Be watchful.* Jesus uses the analogy of the day of the Lord coming like a thief in the night. Just as you wouldn't want a thief to break into your house when you were physically asleep, you wouldn't want Jesus to return when you were spiritually asleep. Jesus tells us:

> "Watch out! Don't let your hearts be dulled by carousing and drunkenness, and by the worries of this life. Don't let that day catch you unaware, like a trap. For that day will come upon everyone living on the earth. Keep alert at all times."
>
> Luke 21:34–35 NLT

As we end this book, we encourage you to heed the last words of Jesus in the Bible: "Yes, I am coming soon." May we all have the same response as John: "Amen. Come, Lord Jesus."

QUESTIONS FOR REFLECTION AND DISCUSSION

- When is the right time to begin preparing for later? Why do we have a tendency to put off that planning?
- What's worse—obsessing over the return of Christ or rarely thinking about it? What is the right balance between these two extremes?
- What is one practical way you can be ready for Christ's return? What about being wise? What does it mean to be spiritually watchful?

Appendix 1

Will There Be Animals in Heaven?

This is a broad question that is easier to answer than you might think. In chapter 9 we talked about a "new heaven" and a "new earth" (Revelation 21:1). Heaven is not just a place "out there," but also a place "down here." Heaven will not only be a spectacular Holy City, but also an incredible "earthly" place of astounding variety and beauty.

The book of Genesis tells us God created the heavens and the earth with an extravagance of flora and fauna (plants and animals) necessary for our survival and enjoyment. The prophet Isaiah declares, "The whole earth is full of his glory" (Isaiah 6:3). Even after the fall, God's glory is evident, though clouded somewhat by sin. But in heaven God's glory will once again be on full display in everything he created (Habakkuk 2:14), including animals.

Even now, animals have a special place in God's creation. As soon as he created people in his own image (Genesis 1:27), he gave them instructions to wisely manage "the fish in the sea and the birds in the sky" and "every living creature that moves on the ground" (verse 28). We humans don't own the animals; they belong to God (Psalm 50:10–11).

Animals were present when God created the first Adam. Animals were present when Jesus, the second Adam, was born. And animals will be present when Jesus, the Lamb of God, is worshiped in heaven (Revelation 5:13).

So yes, there will be animals in heaven. But will *your* animal be in heaven? Your pets—the dogs and cats and horses and whatever kind of animals you cared for like they were part of the family—will they be in heaven?

This is a tougher question to answer. Honestly, we're a little divided on this question. Because Bruce's experience with pets has not been all that positive—his kids once had a dog he affectionately referred to as Satan—he doesn't want his stinky pets to greet him when he gets to heaven. On the other hand, Stan is fond of all the dogs his family has cared for over the years. He would be happy to discover heavenly versions of Trevor, Zoey, and Sammy.

Of course, we can't answer the question of pets in heaven based on our personal preferences. We have to dig a little deeper into Scripture to see if there's any evidence. Unfortunately, there isn't much to go on. The Bible does tell us that God preserves "both people and animals" (Psalm 36:6), but we shouldn't interpret this to mean he preserves them in the same way.

People who have trusted Jesus in this life will be resurrected in the next with new bodies. There's no evidence that animals, including your beloved pets, will be resurrected. It's more likely God will re-create animals who have lived in our present world, or he could create some brand-new animals. We simply don't know how God will do it. We just know it is beyond our ability to imagine, and it will be better than we expect. As Scot McKnight writes,

> In the final Heaven we will see everything that exists in the world, only it will be much better and getting better all the time.[1]

Appendix 2

Can My Loved Ones in Heaven See Me?

We touched on this question in chapter 9, but upon further review, we decided to give you another perspective. Just like the question about animals in heaven, this is a very personal question, even more so when you consider that we are talking about the people we care about most.

This question also goes to the discussion about the "intermediate state"—that period between the time a Christian dies and when Jesus returns (we talked about this in chapter 2). We would like to think that our departed loved ones are not in some kind of suspended animation (some refer to it as *soul sleep*), but are experiencing a conscious, active life with Jesus and perhaps enjoying relationships with other believers, including those they knew during their time on earth.

This is not an unreasonable conclusion, although there's not a lot in Scripture that speaks to the intermediate state. The strongest description is given by Jesus himself, when he says to the repentant thief hanging on a cross next to him, "Truly I tell you, today you will be with me in paradise" (Luke 23:43). Some theologians have suggested this paradise is a mirror image of the original garden of Eden. If that's the case, departed Christians may now be dwelling in a delightful physical place, though not as glorious as the new heaven and new earth described in Revelation 21.

So is paradise a self-contained, closed system, or can the believers who dwell there see what's going on here on earth in real time? While Scripture is sketchy on the topic, there are a couple of passages that seem to indicate an awareness of our present-time activities. We referred to Hebrews 12:1 in chapter 9 and cited the view that the witnesses are merely examples of how to live the Christian life—by faith and with courage. But there is also the view, most notably cited by Randy Alcorn, that the word *surround* should be taken literally, as in we are now surrounded by a great cloud of witnesses. "The imagery seems to suggest that these saints, the spiritual 'athletes' of old, are now watching us and cheering us from the great stadium of Heaven that looks down on the field of Earth," Alcorn writes.[1]

Another passage is found in Revelation 6, where the martyrs in heaven call out to the Lord, "How long . . . until you judge the inhabitants of the earth and avenge our blood?" (verse 10). This seems to indicate an awareness of earth history and events.

But what about all the evil on the earth? Isn't heaven supposed to be a place where there is no more "death or mourning or crying or pain" (Revelation 21:4)? How could the saints in this intermediate heaven not see the bad stuff and have it affect them? Alcorn argues that Jesus is in paradise now, with the saints, and certainly he is aware of all that's going on here on earth—both the good and the bad. Angels come to mind as well. Scripture indicates that they know what's going on (1 Corinthians 4:9; 1 Timothy 5:21).[2]

Maybe it's stretching things just a bit to present such a definite picture on just a few passages, but you're going to be on safe ground to believe that your departed loved ones are aware of you and are cheering you on, that you might "run with perseverance the race marked out" for you.

Appendix 3

Will There Be Rewards in Heaven?

We live in the age of self-esteem. There are no losers, only winners. Even on the losing team, everyone gets a participation trophy. Kids are told they can become anyone and anything they want, as long as they just believe in themselves. Where this comes from is hard to say. Maybe it's our politically correct culture, where everyone's opinion is equally valid and everyone's effort is equally prized. Whatever the reason, this view that everyone's opinion and effort are the same has crept into the church.

Now, we want to be clear that we're not talking about anyone's effort to earn salvation, which is something we are given by God by his grace through faith in Jesus Christ (Ephesians 2:8–9). The effort we're discussing here has to do with rewards in heaven based on our good works.

That's right, the Bible talks about earning rewards through our good works. In fact, good works, while contributing nothing to our salvation, are part of God's plan for us. We are his "handiwork, created in Christ Jesus to do good works, which God prepared in advance for us to do" (Ephesians 2:10).

That's why the apostle Paul hammers this theme home again and again:

- Those who share the gospel with others will "be rewarded according to their own labor" (1 Corinthians 3:8).
- Anything we do for the Lord will not be in vain (1 Corinthians 15:58).
- Whatever we do, we need to work at it with all our hearts, "since you know that you will receive an inheritance from the Lord as a reward" (Colossians 3:24).

Paul's not the only one who emphasizes rewards. In his Sermon on the Mount, Jesus is clear about the value of storing up "treasures in heaven." He tells his followers,

> "But store up for yourselves treasures in heaven, where moths and vermin do not destroy, and where thieves do not break in and steal. For where your treasure is, there your heart will be also."
>
> Matthew 6:20–21

These aren't symbolic treasures, but actual rewards. Paul explains how important it is for believers to build on the foundation of Christ's work for us with works of our own. On the day of judgment, our works will be "revealed with fire, and the fire will test the quality of each person's work" (1 Corinthians 3:13).

What will these rewards look like? Will those whose works pass the test live in bigger mansions (John 14:2 KJV)? Will they get more face time with Moses, Peter, and Paul? We can only speculate. However, what we can safely conclude is that there will be *degrees* of rewards, based on a parable Jesus told about a master who rewarded his productive servants and penalized the lazy ones (Matthew 25:14–30).

Since this parable is given in the context of a talk Jesus gave to his disciples about the end times, the message is clear. Being prepared for the return of Christ requires that we work in a way that produces results. Playing it safe just doesn't cut it.

Appendix 4

Are Near-Death Experiences for Real?

The recent proliferation of books about people who have supposedly died, gone to heaven, and then returned to life with stories of their celestial vacation (the heaven tourism books) makes you wonder if these near-death experiences (NDEs) are for real or figments of overactive imaginations.

If you go by the immense popularity of books like *Heaven Is for Real*, a multimillion-selling book about a boy who dies and goes to heaven and comes back, the least you can say is that people are very curious about this question. They want to know if NDEs are for real, and by implication, if heaven is for real.

Here's our quick response. If the historic words of Jesus, who actually died and came back to life, are not enough to convince someone that heaven is for real, why would the words of a little boy do the trick? Do the subjective words of everyday people carry more weight than the Bible?

Maybe we're being a little harsh. Personal experiences count for something, and millions of such experiences can't be dismissed out of hand. Something is going on. Certainly we don't discount the story of someone who has radically changed because they became a Christian (the churchy word for this is *testimony*). Such stories can be a convincing way for people to see the power of the gospel. We don't question someone's testimony about Jesus setting them free from a life of drug dependency, so why should we doubt the experience of someone who said they saw Jesus in heaven?

In fact, didn't the apostle Paul, when he was still known as Saul and was persecuting Christians with a vengeance, meet Jesus on the road to Damascus in a way that dramatically changed his life (Acts 9)? Even though Saul was the only one who saw the blinding light and heard the voice from heaven calling his name, the Bible doesn't record anyone who doubted his story. They may have wondered if he was a truly changed man, but evidently nobody said of his encounter with the living Christ, "You made that up." By the same token, do we have the right to question the experiences of people who have seen Jesus, whether it's in a dream or in heaven?

The answer is both no and yes. No, we shouldn't automatically doubt someone's experience of coming face-to-face with their own mortality and getting a glimpse of heaven in the process. At the same time, yes, we should be skeptical if that glimpse reveals a heaven that is very different from the heaven described in the Bible.

In fact, when you consider the wide range of stories told by people who have had NDEs, the picture that emerges is one of great variety. Research in this field reveals that the descriptions of what someone sees in their NDE aligns with the belief they had before the experience. A Christian will report seeing heaven and Jesus or loved ones who have departed, while a Hindu will see something quite different.

While the books and films about NDEs and heaven tourism could conceivably convince someone to consider that there's something beyond this life we now experience, there's another more reliable source for these common experiences: God himself. The Bible makes it very clear that God is the reason we think about the afterlife, whether those thoughts come to us in a dream or when we are daydreaming. "He has made everything beautiful in its time," the writer of Ecclesiastes says. "He has also set eternity in the human heart" (Ecclesiastes 3:11).

We think about God because God is real and he made us. We think about life after life and the reality of heaven because that's where God is taking us if we put our trust in him. These thoughts and dreams are but a preview of the reality that is coming in eternity. The reason we know this to be true isn't because someone else went to heaven and back, but because Jesus has made it possible.

Therefore, since we are surrounded by such a great cloud of witnesses, let us throw off everything that hinders and the sin that so easily entangles. And let us run with perseverance the race marked out for us, fixing our eyes on Jesus, the pioneer and perfecter of faith. For the joy set before him he endured the cross, scorning its shame, and sat down at the right hand of the throne of God. Consider him who endured such opposition from sinners, so that you will not grow weary and lose heart.

Hebrews 12:1–3

Notes

Chapter 1: Is There an Afterlife?

1. Alan F. Segal, *Life After Death: A History of the Afterlife in the Religions of the West* (New York: Doubleday, 2004), 699.

2. History.com, "Tombs," 2009, accessed February 20, 2016, http://www.history.com/topics/tombs.

3. Sir Edwin Arnold, trans., *The Bhagavad-Gita*, vol. 45, part 4, ch. 2, The Harvard Classics (New York: P. F. Collier & Son, 1909–1914), accessed April 21, 2016, http://www.bartleby.com/45/4/2.html.

4. Obayashi Hiroshi, *Death and the Afterlife: Perspectives of World Religions* (Westport, CT: Praeger Publishers, 1991), 98.

5. Dinesh D'Souza, *Life After Death: The Evidence* (Washington, D.C.: Regnery, 2009), 125.

6. Ibid., 136.

7. Ibid., 105.

8. Freeman Dyson, *A Many-Colored Glass: Reflections on the Place of Life in the Universe* (Charlottesville, VA: University of Virginia Press, 2010), 76.

9. D'Souza, 106.

10. D'Souza, 74.

11. Jesse Greenspan, "The Myth of Ponce de Leon and the Fountain of Youth," 2013, accessed March 17, 2016, http://www.history.com/news/the-myth-of-ponce-de-leon-and-the-fountain-of-youth.

12. Norman L. Geisler, Ed., *Baker Encyclopedia of Christian Apologetics* (Grand Rapids, MI: 1998), 355.

13. Ibid.

Chapter 2: What Happens When You Die?

1. Daily average calculated from 2,626,418 total deaths in 2014, as reported in Kenneth D. Kochanek, et al., "Deaths: Final Data for 2014," *National Vital Statistics Reports* 64, no. 4 (2016): 1, https://www.cdc.gov/nchs/data/nvsr/nvsr65/nvsr65_04.pdf.

2. Daily average calculated from 3,988,076 total births in 2014, as reported in Brady E. Hamilton, et al., "Births: Final Data for 2014," *National Vital Statistics Reports* 64, no. 12: 2, https://www.cdc.gov/nchs/data/nvsr/nvsr64 /nvsr64_12.pdf.

3. Associated Press, "Two-Thirds of Americans Believe in 'Right to Die,'" May 29, 2007, Fox News, http://www.foxnews.com/story/2007/05/29/two-thirds -americans-believe-in-right-to-die.html.

4. TIME Staff, "TIME Talks to Google CEO Larry Page About Its New Venture to Extend Human Life," TIME Business, September 28, 2013, http://business.time .com/2013/09/18/google-extend-human-life/.

5. Bloomburg News, "Investor Peter Thiel Planning to Live 120 Years," Bloomburg.com, December 18, 2014, https://www.bloomberg.com/news/articles/2014 -12-18/investor-peter-thiel-planning-to-live-120-years.

6. Ariana Eunjung Cha, "Tech Titans' Latest Project: Defy Death," *Washington Post*, April 4, 2015, http://www.washingtonpost.com/sf/national/2015/04/04/tech -titans-latest-project-defy-death/.

Chapter 3: Are Heaven and Hell for Real?

1. Billy Graham, "Did Jesus Ever Say Anything About Hell?," *My Answers*, Billy Graham Evangelistic Association, January 11, 2012, http://billygraham.org /answer/did-jesus-ever-say-anything-about-hell-i-dont-believe-in-hell-myself/.

Chapter 4: Can I Believe What the Bible Says About the End of the World?

1. Dr. Tony Phillips, "Why the World Didn't End Yesterday," NASA Science, December 22, 2012, https://science.nasa.gov/science-news/science-at-nasa/2012 /14dec_yesterday. [Authors' note: We find it interesting that the NASA article was written on December 21, 2012, and released on December 22, 2012; it included the following note at the beginning of the article: "NASA is so sure the world won't come to an end on Dec. 21, 2012, they have already released this news item for the day after."]

2. Reported by Elena Garcia, "Harold Camping Admits He's Wrong About Doomsday Predictions (Full Statement)," *The Christian Post*, March 7, 2012, http:// www.christianpost.com/news/harold-camping-admits-hes-wrong-about-doom sday-predictions-full-statement-71008/.

3. R. C. Sproul, *Essential Truths of the Christian Faith* (Wheaton, IL: Tyndale, 1992), 15–16.

4. Dr. Hugh Ross, "Fulfilled Prophecy: Evidence for the Reliability of the Bible," RTB, 1975, revised by Krista Bontrager, August 22, 2003, http://www.reasons .org/articles/articles/fulfilled-prophecy-evidence-for-the-reliability-of-the-bible.

5. Rich Robinson, "365 Messianic Prophecies," Jews for Jesus, January 15, 2015, http://jewsforjesus.org/answers/prophecy/365-messianic-prophecies.

6. Peter W. Stoner, *Science Speaks: Scientific Proof of the Accuracy of the Prophecy and the Bible*, online edition, 2005, chapter 3, http://sciencespeaks. dstoner.net/Christ_of_Prophecy.html#c9.

7. Ibid.

Chapter 5: Do All Roads Lead to Heaven?

1. Timothy Keller, *Encounters with Jesus: Unexpected Answers to Life's Biggest Questions* (New York: Dutton, 2013), 193.

2. Peter Kreeft, *Everything You Ever Wanted to Know About Heaven . . . But Never Dreamed of Asking* (San Francisco: Ignatius Press, 1990), 243.

3. Ibid., 245.

4. Ibid.

5. Ibid., 246.

6. C. S. Lewis, *Mere Christianity* (New York: Simon & Schuster, 1996), 56.

7. Kreeft, 246.

8. Ibid.

9. Ibid., 242.

10. Lee Strobel, *The Case for the Real Jesus: A Journalist Investigates Current Attacks on the Identity of Christ* (Grand Rapids, MI: Zondervan, 2007), 250.

11. Ibid., 250–251.

12. Barry Corey, "Firm Centers and Soft Edges," *Biola Magazine* (Summer 2014), http://magazine.biola.edu/article/14-summer/firm-centers-and-soft-edges/.

13. Scot McKnight, *The Heaven Promise: Engaging the Bible's Truth About Life to Come* (Colorado Springs, CO: Waterbrook Press, 2015), 160.

14. R. Douglas Geivett, "Is Jesus the Only Way?" in *Jesus Under Fire: Modern Scholarship Reinvents the Historical Jesus*, ed. Michael J. Wilkins and J. P. Moreland (Grand Rapids, MI: Zondervan, 1995), 199.

15. Ibid.

16. Philip Yancey, *Where Is God When It Hurts?* (Grand Rapids, MI: Zondervan, 1997), 160.

Chapter 6: If God Is Loving, How Could He Send Anyone to Hell?

1. Abbreviated and paraphrased for publication purposes.

2. David L. Edwards and John Stott, *Evangelical Essentials: A Liberal-Evangelical Dialogue* (London: Hodder & Stoughton, 1988), 313.

3. Martin E. Marty, "Hell Disappeared. No One Noticed. A Civic Argument," *The Harvard Theological Review*, 78, no. 3/4 (July–October, 1985): 393.

4. Mike Anton and William Lobdell, "Hold the Fire and Brimstone," *Los Angeles Times*, June 19, 2002.

5. Ibid., quoting Bruce Shelley, senior professor of church history at Denver Seminary.

6. John F. MacArthur, *Parables: The Mysteries of God's Kingdom Revealed through the Stories Jesus Told* (Nashville: Thomas Nelson, 2015), Kindle edition, chapter 9.

7. Albert Mohler, "Modern Theology: The Disappearance of Hell," in *Hell under Fire: Modern Scholarship Reinvents Eternal Punishment*, ed. Christopher W. Morgan and Robert A. Peterson (Grand Rapids, MI: Zondervan, 2004), quoting from Geerhardus Vos, "The Scriptural Doctrine of the Love of God" in *Redemptive History and Biblical Interpreation: The Shorter Writings of Geerhardus Vos*, ed. Richard B. Gaffin (Grand Rapids, MI: Baker, 1980 [1902]), 426.

8. *Urban Dictionary*, s.v. "millennial," accessed December 20, 2016, www .UrbanDictionary.com/define.php?term=Millennial.

9. Nathaniel Branden, *The Psychology of Self-Esteem: A Revolutionary Approach to Self-Understanding That Launched a New Era in Modern Psychology* (San Francisco: Jossey-Bass, 2001 [1969]), 250.

10. Po Bronson, "How Not to Talk to Your Kids: The Inverse Power of Praise," *New York* magazine, August 3, 2007, http://nymag.com/news/features/27840/.

11. Melanie Phillips, "Everybody Wins and All Must Have Prizes," *Daily Mail*, September 22, 2003, http://www.dailymail.co.uk/columnists/article-229966/Time -stop-classwar-ideologues.html.

12. "Children, obey your parents in the Lord, for this is right." Ephesians 6:1

13. Edwards and Stott, *Evangelical Essentials*, 313.

14. R. C. Sproul, *The Holiness of God* (Wheaton, IL: Tyndale, 1985), 40.

15. Ibid., 55.

16. Ibid., 54.

Chapter 7: Is Hell a Divine Torture Chamber?

1. Douglas J. Moo, *The NIV Application Commentary: 2 Peter, Jude* (Grand Rapids, MI: Zondervan, 1977), 262.

2. Sproul, *Essential Truths*, 297.

3. Moo, *NIV Application Commentary*, 264.

4. Douglas J. Moo, "Paul on Hell," in *Hell under Fire*, ed. Morgan and Peterson, 104–105.

5. Rob Bell, *Love Wins: A Book About Heaven, Hell, and the Fate of Every Person Who Ever Lived* (New York: HarperOne, 2011), 107.

6. J. I. Packer, "Universalism: Will Everyone Ultimately Be Saved?" in *Hell under Fire*, ed. Morgan and Peterson, 157.

7. See Francis Chan and Preston Sprinkle, *Erasing Hell: What God Said About Eternity, and the Things We've Made Up* (Colorado Springs: David C. Cook, 2011), 24–25.

8. MacArthur, *Parables*, appendix.

9. Ibid.

10. C. S. Lewis, *The Great Divorce* (New York: The Macmillan Company, 1973), 77–78.

Chapter 8: How Do You Get into Heaven?

1. *The Christian Post* "Traditional Beliefs Still Intact," October 28, 2003, http:// www.christianpost.com/news/traditional-beliefs-still-intact-19826/.

2. Randy Alcorn, *Heaven* (Carol Stream, IL: Tyndale, 2004), 31–32.

3. Cornelius Plantinga Jr., *Not the Way It's Supposed to Be: A Breviary on Sin* (Grand Rapids, MI: Eerdmans, 1995), 7.

4. Ibid., 10.

5. Ibid., 16.

6. Francis Spufford, *Unapologetic: Why, Despite Everything, Christianity Can Still Make Surprising Emotional Sense* (San Francisco: HarperOne, 2014), 16.

Chapter 9: What Will Heaven Be Like?

1. reh3959, "40 Movies Dealing in Some Way with the Afterlife," Internet Movie Database, May 18, 2011, http://www.imdb.com/list/ls000680623/.
2. Scot McKnight, "10 Things I Wish Everyone Knew About Heaven," FaithStreet.com, October 6, 2015, http://www.faithstreet.com/onfaith/2015/10/06/10-things-i-wish-everyone-knew-about-heaven/37890.
3. Sproul, *Essential Truths*, 279.
4. Wayne Grudem, *Systematic Theology: An Introduction to Biblical Doctrine* (Grand Rapids, MI: Zondervan, 1994), 1,163.
5. McKnight, "10 Things I Wish Everyone Knew About Heaven."
6. Quoted in Alcorn, *Heaven*, 168.
7. Ibid., 282.
8. McKnight, "10 Things I Wish Everyone Knew About Heaven."
9. Grudem, *Systematic Theology*, 1,164.
10. C. S. Lewis, *Letters to Malcolm: Chiefly on Prayer* (New York: Harcourt, Brace and World, 1964), 124.

Chapter 10: How Can I Be Sure About Heaven?

1. Alcorn, *Heaven*, 35.
2. Dallas Willard, *The Divine Conspiracy: Rediscovering Our Hidden Life in God* (San Francisco: HarperSanFrancisco, 1998), 366.
3. Ibid., 367.
4. Ibid., 367–369.
5. C. S. Lewis, "The World's Last Night," in *Fern-Seed and Elephants and Other Essays on Christianity* (New York: HarperCollins, 1998), 62.
6. Ibid., 64.
7. Ibid.
8. Bruce Bickel and Stan Jantz, *Revelation: Unlocking the Mysteries of the End Times* (Eugene, OR: Harvest House, 2003), 165–166.

Appendix 1: Will There Be Animals in Heaven?

1. Scot McKnight, *The Heaven Promise*, 186.

Appendix 2: Can My Loved Ones in Heaven See Me?

1. Alcorn, *Heaven*, 70.
2. Ibid., 70–73.

After graduating from college as a theater arts major, **Bruce Bickel** entered the entertainment industry as a standup comedian. But his show-biz career was short-lived because he wasn't very funny. Like most failing comedians, he became a lawyer—a profession in which he is considered hilarious. Bruce preaches sermons quite often (but never at a church, just in his spare bedroom).

Stan Jantz has spent his entire professional career selling, publishing, and writing Christian books. Writing is his favorite book activity, because he gets to do it with his longtime coauthor, Bruce Bickel. Together Bruce and Stan have written 75 books with more than 3.5 million copies sold. They have plenty of spare time to write because neither of them has a hobby (much to the chagrin of their wives).

When he's not writing, Stan serves as the executive director of the Evangelical Christian Publishers Association. He loves this job because he gets to spend time with publishing leaders who have the audacity to think they can change the world through Christ-centered books. Stan thinks they may be on to something.

More From Bruce Bickel and Stan Jantz

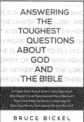

In a thoughtful, candid way, this book asks the big questions: *Is God real and how can I know? Does God really care about me and my life?* While some answers are provided, there is enough space and grace for you to wrestle, doubt, and dig deeper.

Answering the Toughest Questions About God and the Bible
by Bruce Bickel and Stan Jantz
conversantlife.com

BETHANY HOUSE

Stay up to date on your favorite books and authors with our free e-newsletters. Sign up today at bethanyhouse.com.

Find us on Facebook. facebook.com/BHPnonfiction

Follow us on Twitter. @bethany_house